CAREERS
F O R
NIGHT OWLS
& Other Insomniacs

VGM Careers for You Series

CAREERS
FOR
NIGHT
OWLS
& Other
Insomniacs

Louise Miller

 **VGM Career Horizons**
a division of *NTC Publishing Group*
Lincolnwood, Illinois USA

Library of Congress Cataloging-in-Publication Data

Miller, Louise
    Careers for night owls and other insomniacs / Louise Miller.
        p. cm.
    Includes bibliographical references.
    ISBN 0-8442-4115-6 (hard) -- ISBN 0-8442-4116-4 (soft)
    1. Vacational guidance. 2. Night work. 3. Night people–
Vocational guidance. I. Title.
    HF5382.M52 1995
    331.7'02--dc20   94-28733
                                                                CIP

Published by VGM Career Horizons, a division of NTC Publishing Group
4255 West Touhy Avenue
Lincolnwood (Chicago), Illinois 60646-1975, U.S.A.

4 5 6 7 8 9 0 VP 9 8 7 6 5 4 3 2 1

Contents

About the Author   vi

CHAPTER ONE
Introduction   1

CHAPTER TWO
The Transportation Industry   10

CHAPTER THREE
The Hospitality Industry   30

CHAPTER FOUR
The Health Care Industry   48

CHAPTER FIVE
The Communications Industry   78

CHAPTER SIX
The Entertainment Industry   106

CHAPTER SEVEN
Security and Social Services   133

CHAPTER EIGHT
Other Night Owl Careers   153

Acknowledgments and Additional Resources   170

About the Author

L ouise Miller is something of a night owl herself since she is presently teaching English on a split shift. She also understands what it means to burn the midnight oil by writing, editing, and researching as a free-lancer. This night owl spirit comes from her love of languages, especially English and German. She started out as a German teacher and teaches it today, after having studied in Vienna, Austria, and Bonn, Germany. She has taught German at universities in Kansas, Missouri, and Illinois.

Her love of English led her to teaching and publishing. She has taught English at community and business colleges, has conducted writing workshops, and has worked both full time and free-lance for various publishing houses. These include New Horizons Publishers, Compton's Encyclopedia, Rand McNally & Company, Richard D. Irwin, and World Book. Miller was also research coordinator for television quiz shows in Los Angeles and has written three books on careers—two on careers for animal lovers and one for those who want to work with nature. She also has written a regular wildlife column for the Woodstock (Illinois) *Sentinel*.

To Charles, a dear friend who enhanced our lives
immeasurably with his generosity, kindness,
and understanding and who will always be remembered.

CHAPTER ONE

Introduction

When most people are growing up and thinking about working for a living, they probably envision themselves in an office working from 9 to 5. It may never occur to them that their hours could be 5 to 9. Sometime after the invention of electricity, however, night became day and vice versa for many workers in the Industrial Age. Even though the Earth turns on its axis every 24 hours and we humans have adapted our lives to that cycle, the world suddenly was turned around and whole new work shifts became possible.

Many jobs have traditionally been conducted on a 24-hour basis. Medical personnel, factory workers, police officers, fire fighters, transportation workers, and emergency road crews have had to be available all day and all night. Today, however, more and more career possibilities are available that fool not only the clock on the wall but also our natural biological clocks.

These nonstandard work schedules, often called shift work, probably involve about 20 million Americans today. Some companies may have three shifts, running 24 hours a day, seven days a week. Others have split shifts; that is, employees work part of their shift in the morning, have an afternoon break, and finish their shift at night. Still others have rotating shifts. For a few days they work during the day and for a few days they work during the night. Those who work the night shift exclusively are said to work the "graveyard" shift. All these possibilities exist in the real work world, and we will explore how they might affect the work that you are considering.

For example, anyone who lives in a big city knows that some services are available all night long. Waiters, cashiers, and attendants are needed for all-night restaurants, laundromats, convenience stores, and gas stations. Police officers and fire fighters, as well as emergency snow crews, security guards, housekeepers, and cab and bus drivers, keep cities running smoothly at all hours. Doctors, nurses, and paramedics, along with ambulance drivers and veterinarians, make sure that humans and animals get the health care that they need at any time of day or night. Hotline operators, social workers, and psychologists may be on call 24 hours.

Without pilots, flight attendants, mechanics, baggage handlers, and air traffic controllers working through the night, we would miss our early morning business meeting, our parents' anniversary, our daughter's wedding, or the morning mail. Truck drivers haul goods across country overnight so that we are fed and clothed; trains and buses run on an all-night schedule transporting goods and people. Drivers, engineers, porters, and waiters are needed for these jobs. Food-service personnel such as bakers work during the night so we can enjoy a fresh croissant with our morning coffee.

When we finally arrive at our destination after the late flight or train ride, we are happy that hotel managers, door people, bell persons, front desk clerks, housekeepers, and room service personnel are there to greet us, no matter how late it is. We may want to go out on the town, to a theater, nightclub, disco, bar, or concert. The actors, musicians, singers, dancers, bartenders, and waiters are there to entertain, feed, and serve us into the wee, small hours of the morning. Or maybe we'd rather go to an all-night movie house. There we'd find ticket agents, ushers, projectionists, night managers, and someone to sell us popcorn—at 5 A.M! Perhaps we're too tired to go out, and we decide to stay in the room and watch television or listen to the radio. Producers, directors, reporters, camera crews, deejays, and talk-show hosts are there to help us get to sleep or to make staying awake more enjoyable.

At breakfast, we will, of course, want to read the early edition of the local newspaper. How did it get there? Thanks to a group of reporters, photographers, writers, editors, word processors, printers, and delivery people who work all hours of the day and night, that's how.

Lawyers involved in a tough court case often work through the night in order to be prepared for the courtroom the next day. Working with them may be a team of paralegals, word processors, and proofreaders. They may send documents out to an all-night print shop where they are printed and bound for the next day. Teachers, especially in adult education programs, may work the morning and evening shifts. Military personnel work rotating shifts all over the world.

After that overview it may seem as if the whole world is doing shift work. That's not the case, but from now on when we see ourselves working for a living, we may not see exclusively the 9-to-5 shift. We know now that much of the work that is done during the day also has to be done during the night. Any one of us may be called upon to work different shifts during our working lives. It could be only temporary or we could decide that it's the only way we want to spend our work life. We may not be able to make up our minds until we actually try shift work, but there are some factors to consider, based on research and other people's experiences.

Advantages and Disadvantages of Night Owl Jobs

Those who work a graveyard, split, or rotating shift know the advantages and disadvantages of working nonstandard hours. Some of the advantages are that you don't have a lot of supervisors around at night, the phones are not constantly ringing to distract you from your work, the usual clients and vendors don't show up at night, and often you will enjoy a relaxed dress code (jeans, T-shirts, and gym shoes may be fine at night but taboo in daylight hours). Perhaps most significant, you may receive a pay differential for working graveyard.

People who work off hours also don't have to face rush-hour traffic. They can schedule doctor and dentist appointments during the day. Grocery shopping goes faster on weekdays than on Saturdays or Sundays because fewer people are shopping then. Department stores, cleaners, restaurants, car washes—all services are more accessible on weekdays.

However, unless you plan carefully, your social and family life may suffer, since the majority of people still work during the day and play at night. Your sleeping and eating habits may change radically—you could be eating breakfast in the evening and having a cocktail before dinner at 8 A.M. Sometimes sleeping during the day is not easy because of street noises and, of course, the sunlight streaming through the windows, even with the shades down and curtains drawn.

Some research also indicates that working nonstandard hours may have some adverse effects on health, and even safety, because our bodies have certain biological rhythms that are close to the 24-hour rotation of the Earth on its axis. These rhythms are referred to as circadian rhythms, and shift work can disrupt them. Your temperature, memory, and awareness can be affected, as well as your sleeping and eating habits.

More research has yet to be done, but some patterns have emerged in the limited research that has been conducted. For instance, there may be a tendency to have more gastrointestinal and cardiovascular disease, as well as reproductive problems—ranging from low birth weight, early births, and miscarriages due to hormonal disruptions—for shift workers. Shift workers may be more prone to accidents, too. Adverse health effects are, of course, highly individual. Some people suffer fatigue and, therefore, lower productivity, but others thrive on night work.

Some studies indicate that the use of bright lights in the workplace and total darkness when sleeping or taking naps, and even some supervised use of drugs, can help night owls adjust their biological clocks. Also, if shifts are rotating, they should be rotated in a clockwise direction. That means that they should be shifted from day to evening to night rather than in the opposite, or counterclockwise, direction. Others recommend that shifts not be changed in less than 10-day increments and that shift workers be given at least 48 hours off between shift changes. It's also a good idea to be on the same shift for at least three weeks before another shift change takes place.

People who work rotating or night shift often feel lonely or isolated, at least in the beginning, because they realize that their family and friends are not available for socializing when they get off work. Special events must be planned carefully because shift workers are often scheduled for nights on holidays, graduation days, birthdays, and anniversaries. If they have schedules in advance, family and friends may adjust these celebrations to meet shift workers' special needs. For example, Christmas could be celebrated on the previous or following weekend rather than on the 25th. The graduation party could be scheduled for a date other than the actual graduation, and even birthday parties can be shifted to accommodate mom's or dad's schedule. Most people are willing to make these adjustments just to have the pleasure of loved ones' company at these special times.

Shift workers also might want to "practice" adjusting to a new shift by gradually going to sleep and getting up later than usual for a while before the change occurs. Before sleeping, it's a good idea to cut down on caffeine, alcohol, sugar, and heavy meals, thereby getting a night of uninterrupted sleep. If your job involves life-and-death situations, such as doctors, police officers, fire fighters, military personnel, or transportation workers, regulating your sleep patterns is essential for the safety of all concerned—you, the patient, victim, or passenger.

People who work at night have to be creative, independent, flexible, and have a sense of humor to get them through the night. They also have to love the work that they do. It also helps if their work involves some variety and they are allowed to take frequent breaks and even naps if possible. As more co-ordinated research is done about our circadian rhythms and how they affect our work life, including productivity and safety, as well as our emotional and social life, the more we will be prepared to do the work we love at any time of day or night.

And that is really the first step we all have to take in choosing a career—finding out what we love to do and how to do it. Since many jobs are now performed at night or at least in non-standard hours, we have to carefully analyze what we really like to do and where our capabilities lie. We can do that by reading, by talking to people who perform those jobs that appeal to us, by doing voluntary or part-time work in that field, or by taking aptitude tests through school placement centers or career counselors.

We should also contact professional organizations, colleges, and universities to see what their requirements are for admittance into the field we are pursuing.

Since we will be exploring a wide variety of career possibilities, you will see that, for some, very little or no previous training or education is necessary. On-the-job training and a few years' experience will give you the opportunity for advancement. For other careers, a great deal of formal education and experience will be necessary.

It's also a good idea to look into the possibilities of working for the military, the government, or private industry before you land on your final career goal. Each of these categories will have different requirements, some stricter than others. The earlier you check out these requirements, the more carefully you will be able to chart your educational course. If you're still in high school, you'll find out whether communication, math, science, or computer skills are more important for your chosen career. You'll see what testing and application procedures are necessary to get the job. You'll discover whether there are opportunities for volunteer work, summer jobs, or apprenticeships available in the field. You'll also see which of your personal qualities or characteristics is most desirable for this job: independence, flexibility, sense of humor, adaptability, or cooperation.

Some jobs will require you to take extensive oral and written examinations, adhere to strict physical requirements, pass psychological and drug tests, and submit to hands-on simulations of the real job. Some jobs require apprenticeships, licenses, certifications, and internships.

Other jobs require manual dexterity; still others require wit and problem-solving skills. Some will demand postgraduate work; others need only a high school diploma. For some, you will need to follow strict rules of applying for the job; for others, answering an ad in the newspaper will get you the job.

As you explore jobs that are available to you with shift work, take a good look at your aptitudes. For example, you may decide that working the graveyard shift is for you. You also heard that many companies hire proofreaders to work through the night. It just so happens, though, that you never did well in English, don't know whether you should use a comma or a semi-colon, and have a terrible spelling problem. At this point, you either have to take some remedial courses—or decide to do something else!

Whichever career choice you make that may involve weird shifts and crazy hours, be prepared for an adventure in a topsy-turvy world where 5 P.M. is starting time and 9 P.M. means quitting time. Your circadian rhythms will be turned upside down. The Earth may revolve counterclockwise, but if you're doing what you love, it doesn't matter what time it is.

We are about to explore many career paths that can be performed during the day, in the evening, or overnight. We will cover careers in transportation, including airlines, buses, trains, and cabs. The hospitality industry also offers a variety of night owl and rotating-shift careers, including hotel managers, waiters, and chefs.

We'll also take a look at health-care possibilities, including physicians, physician assistants, nurses, paramedics, and technicians—the careers that have traditionally been geared to night owls.

The expanding world of communications will provide you with many opportunities for shift work, rotating shifts, and graveyard work. These jobs will include newspapers, radio, TV, telecommunications, and the very real and emerging career possibilities in cyberspace and interactive news and entertainment. Cable TV, computers, networks, and a whole range of on-line possibilities will also be discussed.

We will also discuss those very important careers that provide for our security in various ways, such as police officers, fire fighters, and security guards. And finally, we will try to wrap up various career possibilities that are involved with shift work. All of these careers are essential in some way or another and will require various degrees of education or training.

We have also included interviews with real people with real night owl jobs with real experience. If you listen to them and to your heart, you will find the career of your choice, and it won't matter whether you get all the sleep you want. You'll just enjoy the work you do. So let's jump in and see which careers might interfere with our sleep, social life, and holidays—the careers for night owls.

For Further Information

American Health Care Association
Information Resource Center
1201 L St., NW
Washington, D.C. 20005

Chronicle Guidance Publications, Inc.
P.O. Box 1190
Moravia, NY 13118

Publications

"Biological Rhythms: Implications for the Worker." OTA Biological Brief,
   Superintendent of Documents, U.S. Government Printing Office,
   Washington, D.C. 20402-9325, September 1991.
Occupational Outlook Handbook, compiled by the U.S. Department of
   Labor, VGM Career Horizons, NTC Publishing Group, Lincolnwood,
   IL (annual).

CHAPTER TWO

The Transportation Industry

All of us have to get somewhere at some time. If you need to be somewhere else in the morning, chances are that you will be traveling at night. Wheels and wings will get you wherever you have to go, with the aid of pilots, flight attendants, cab and bus drivers, engineers, and conductors. If goods have to be shipped across country, truck drivers will be driving through the night. Cab and bus drivers work the city streets when most of us are sleeping. Traveling overseas by boat requires the captain of the ship and a crew who will also be working at night.

Night Owl Careers in Air Travel

Let's first take a look at the people who make an airline run, what they do, and when they do it. Basically, every commercial airline has a captain who is the chief pilot, responsible for all safety aspects of the flight. Alongside the captain is the copilot, who is second in command to the captain. The second officer or flight engineer sees to the mechanical and electronic functions of the aircraft, and the flight attendants oversee the safety and comfort of the passengers. A flight dispatcher determines when the aircraft may take off and land and monitors the flight to its final destination.

All airspace in the United States is regulated by the Federal Aviation Administration (FAA). This means that the FAA is responsible for the safety of half a billion passengers a year in approximately 200,000 takeoffs and landings. Anyone who operates or maintains aircraft has to be certified by the FAA. This includes pilots, dispatchers, and, at this writing, air traffic control specialists. There is, however, pending legislation to remove air traffic control specialists from FCC control.

Pilots

There are five categories of pilots:

1. Student

2. Recreational

3. Private

4. Commercial

5. Airline transport

Pilots are rated according to the category and class of aircraft that they fly. Commercial pilots are hired by airlines to transport passengers and cargo to and from destinations throughout the world.

The top job in a commercial airline is the captain, but you don't get to be captain overnight—it takes years of service as a pilot after years of thorough training and certification.

In order to become a pilot, you first have to get a commercial pilot's license and FAA certification. You have to be at least 18 years old and have flown at least 250 hours. You will have to pass a thorough physical examination, have 20/20 vision, and pass a written examination. Then FAA examiners actually test your flying ability. The physical and flying exams have to be repeated periodically in order to keep your license valid.

To become a flight engineer for an airline, you have to pass further FAA exams, and to become a captain, you have to have an airline transport pilot's license. For this, you have to be at least 23 years old and have flown at least 1,500 hours. You can get an FAA rating for bad-weather, night, and instrument flying with further testing and flying demonstrations.

Many people start flying during their military training, while others learn at colleges, universities, or private flying schools. About 600 flying schools around the country have already received FAA certification. You will have to have at least a high school diploma to become a commercial pilot, but more and more airlines are looking for college graduates for these positions.

Average annual earnings for commercial airline pilots in 1990 were about $80,000; copilots, $65,000; flight engineers, $40,000; and captains, $107,000. The job outlook into the 21st century looks good because of expected growth in transportation needs.

Flight Attendants

If you walk out of the cockpit into the cabin of the plane, you walk into the world of the flight attendant. It is here that the flight attendants' work is done, even before passengers board the plane. That's when they prepare the cabin for flight by seeing to food and beverage supplies, reading materials, pillows, blankets, and first aid kits. As passengers board, the attendants collect tickets and assist passengers with storing luggage, locating their seats, and caring for their special needs.

Since one of the most important functions of the flight attendants is the passengers' safety, they also are required to give visual instructions on what passengers should do in an emergency. If one actually occurs, they make sure that the emergency exits are open and that the chutes are inflated for evacuation. They also make sure that passengers' seat belts are fastened and that their seats are upright before takeoff and during landing. During the flight, attendants serve food and beverages, help passengers who need special care, and administer first aid as needed. When the plane lands, they help passengers out of the plane. After the flight, they often have to write reports, collect items left behind, and generally check the condition of the cabin.

If you want to become a flight attendant, you will have to be at least 19 to 21 years old for most commercial airlines and a high school graduate. Any further education or experience dealing with the public is a plus.

If you decide to work for an international airline, you will also have to speak the pertinent foreign language fluently. Your health and communication skills have to be excellent as an attendant because you will be on your feet most of the time, the work can be stressful, and you always have to be congenial with the passengers.

You will also have to be prepared for an irregular schedule, often working holidays, weekends, and overnight. You will probably fly on the average 80 hours a month and be on the ground the same number of hours. If you have to stay overnight in another city, the airline provides a hotel room and meals.

If you are hired as a flight attendant, you will be trained for four to six weeks. You will learn all the responsibilities, rules and regulations, and policies and procedures for this demanding job. After that, you will be assigned to a home base where you will get regular assignments for one to five years. In the meantime, you will probably be on reserve status.

Recent salary figures for entry-level positions are $13,000 annually; with six years' experience, $20,000; and for senior flight attendants, $35,000. You and your family will receive discounts on fares, and some attendants are paid more for night flights. Flight attendants can move up to become senior flight attendants or flight attendant supervisors. They can also become flight attendant instructors, customer service directors, or recruiting representatives.

Flight dispatchers work with the pilot to provide a flight plan with maximum cargo and passengers at the lowest cost. In order to do this, the dispatcher has to evaluate weather conditions in the air and at the destination city, judge how much fuel will be needed, and analyze traffic flow. The dispatcher has to be aware of all dispatched flights and report to both the pilot and personnel on the ground. They have to know all routes and facilities at the airport and the takeoff and landing capabilities of all appropriate aircraft.

Air Traffic Controllers

Without air traffic controllers, no flight would be safe—day or night. These highly trained specialists help to determine the arrivals and departures of all civilian and military flights. As such, they are essential for national defense and civilian safety. Controllers can be employed by the FAA, the Department of Defense (DOD), local or state governments, or private airlines.

There are three kinds of air traffic control specialists:

1. Terminal area air traffic controller,

2. En route air traffic controller, and

3. Flight service specialist.

Terminal area air traffic controllers supply the pilot with weather conditions, takeoff and landing clearance, and information about other aircraft approaching, leaving, or flying through the airport. They use radio, radar, or visual observation to make sure that planes are a safe distance from each other in the air and on the runway. Radar can detect planes at least

40 miles from the airport, which will allow for a safe landing and departure.

En route controllers are FAA employees who work in centers located throughout the country. They take the aircraft, operating according to instrument flight rules, through the airspace from airport to airport. They transmit weather and traffic information to the pilots, and pilots transmit their positions along the way. They can also ask for a change in route or altitude during the flight.

Flight services specialists are responsible for preflight information about weather and general airport conditions. They send the pilot's flight plan to the air traffic controller and to the flight service station at the destination airport.

To become an air traffic control specialist, you have to be at least 18 years old, have excellent oral communications skills, and pass a very strict physical examination. You can enroll for training programs through the Army, Navy, Air Force, or the FAA/Department of Transportation (DOT). You will definitely get a job as a controller if you successfully complete the academic program of the FAA/DOT, but you will need two to four years of training to become fully qualified as a controller.

The work itself is demanding and requires rotating shift work because air travel is available 24 hours a day, year-round. The shifts will vary depending on the individual facility's work load and traffic patterns. Those controllers working for the FAA/DOT or the Department of Defense (DOD) receive more pay when they work Sundays, holidays, or nights.

The federal government has rather strict rules for applying for jobs in all its departments, including the FAA. Federal jobs are classified by grades, from 1 to 10, based on the level of difficulty and responsibility of that job. Each state has an Office of Personnel Job Information Placement Center which you can contact for job availability information, but your application form (SF171) should be sent directly to the FAA.

At the airport, you will also find ticket agents who figure out fares, write tickets, check in baggage, and answer questions about departures and arrivals. The skycaps help you with your luggage, and food service employees make sure you have something to eat during the flight. Baggage handlers will make sure you get your luggage after the flight.

All these careers have shift work built in. They include rotating shifts and graveyard shifts. So if you'd like to be involved in the travel industry, there are ample opportunities for you to choose from—and to become a night owl.

Profile of a Flight Attendant

Vicki McIntyre-Brezinski has been a flight attendant for United Airlines for 23 years, and she has worked every shift the airline has to offer.

Irregular hours are not strange to Vicki, whose father was a pilot with different hours of work each week and each month. Vicki grew up with a positive image of these crazy hours, because, after all, her father's job provided the family with food and clothing—and travel privileges. Life was more casual, especially at mealtime, when her father was working. However, they were much more formal when he was home because it was a rare event.

Holidays were often celebrated later in her home than the actual date. So after she and her friends had already played with their toys for a few days after Christmas, she was just receiving her new ones. She learned to like this system and realized that she did not identify with people who lived for the weekend and had to celebrate holidays strictly on that day. In other words, she learned flexibility at an early age.

Vicki did not consciously pursue an alternate work style, but she certainly did not resist it. She was always encouraged to try everything, even though it might be different from what everyone else did. Actually, Vicki started out as a musician—a drummer. This was unusual for a female, but she played in combos in high school and college, loved the applause, and became addicted to the night life-style.

She was playing with a band in Hawaii but had to return home for treatment of a kidney ailment. During that time, the band broke up. She did not want to sign up with an agent, but she did want some job security. The airline offered security and a possible chance to return to Hawaii.

She was hired as a clerk in dispatch with honest-to-goodness rotating shift work. Vicki was working one week of mornings, one week of nights, and one week of afternoons, "on" six days, "off" two. The dispatchers had done it for years, and she fell in love with it. She loved not having to fight rush-hour traffic and crowded stores.

After a year as a clerk, Vicki was hired as a flight attendant. Although it was probably more her parents' dream than her own, she thought that she might, as a flight attendant, get to Hawaii to reestablish her musical connections.

As luck would have it, the airline wanted to use both her skills and allowed her to participate in musical road shows for the airline to raise morale for other employees. This experience made Vicki realize that she had made a successful transition from music to a profession with more security and benefits than that of a musician.

Vicki had the opportunity to work 9 to 5, both as a flight attendant instructor and in-flight sales representative. But this lasted only six months, and she was transferred to a ground supervisor position with regular hours. Within months, she was miserable. She hated the rush-hour traffic, the crowded stores, and the repetition of the work—seeing the same faces every day. Although she did it for a year, she cried every day during the last three months that she had the job.

Vicki seems to be made for the night shift. She is now an international flight attendant and flies mostly at night, and that makes her very happy because passengers are simply less demanding when they are asleep! But the attraction to night work for Vicki is still the diversity of the changing schedules, coworkers, and customers.

Even Vicki admits that after 23 years, the duties become routine. Therefore, she has to face the challenge of not slipping into complacency, especially in regards to the passengers. She does that with a large dose of empathy—she puts herself into the passengers' shoes and tries to make them as comfortable as she would like to be. Also, her sense of humor allows her the freedom of entertaining a built-in audience and the knowledge that she will never see the disagreeable ones again.

The only frustration that Vicki has working her strange and rotating hours is trying to function in a society that thinks 9 to 5 is normal. For instance, she finds it hard to get a doctor's or dentist's appointment when she doesn't know her schedule for the following month until the 20th of the previous month. Sometimes the only appointment available is for 10 A.M. when she has just arrived home at 5 A.M. When she has a series of trips, it's difficult to find grocery stores, cleaners, and department stores to match her weird hours, even though there are more 24-hour facilities available now than ever before. It is also difficult trying to manage a social life with people who work "straight" hours, including having all weekends off.

After many years as a single woman, Vicki recently married a television editor who also has very irregular work hours. Luckily they understand the unpredictability of each other's jobs. But in the process, Vicki has also inherited a family who initially couldn't understand why she might not be around for the scheduled holidays.

She also has a newborn child, and it may be difficult to find child care since her husband has to be at work at 6 A.M. Vicki may look to hire a retired person who is available for in-home child care because retirees do not have fixed schedules and welcome a fixed income for their services.

Jet lag and time zone changes are also challenges for international travelers. Vicki thinks that you really never overcome it; you just learn to adjust to it. You also can't possibly try to combine regular and irregular hours to keep up a social life. You will only become dysfunctional from exhaustion. It takes Vicki about a day or two to adjust to being home after a long trip. Luckily her family gives her the time and space to recuperate in her own way.

Even though she does experience some hardships with her alternate life-style, Vicki wouldn't change it. But some things definitely make it easier for her. For example, she cites 24-hour shopping facilities, cellular phones, and increasing acceptance of the 5 to 9 schedule by those who work more traditional hours than ever before.

Vicki thinks that with the growing population in this country, coupled with the advent of the communications superhighway and high-tech advances, many companies will have more in-home workers. Alternative work hours will have to overlap somewhat with traditional ones, and if these "abnormal" work shifts become more "normal," additional pay will not be offered for the graveyard shift.

Until that time comes, Vicki is very happy with her odd hours. She feels that those who work alternate hours are independent, flexible, and adventurous. And Vicki seems to fit that glove very well.

Night Owl Careers in Land Transportation

Back on land, we need bus, cab, and truck drivers, as well as railroad workers to move us around to hotels, offices, and restaurants and to deliver food, beverages, medicine, furniture, and all manner of goods that we need for our daily lives. Night work is necessary for all these jobs.

Bus Drivers and Truckers

Some bus drivers work for private companies and transport people within a state or across country. Municipal bus drivers provide transportation for all those workers who have the graveyard shift or for those who are out on the town.

Long-haul truck drivers can be away from home overnight, or they might be driving all week, with stops for food, rest, refueling, and unloading. Sometimes they have a regular run; other times, dispatchers inform them where to go next. At the end of the run, the drivers have to fill in reports on the trip, including details of any accidents. This is required by the Department of Transportation (DOT).

The DOT regulates all trucking companies that deal in interstate commerce regarding work hours for the drivers. Individual states also have standards for truck drivers, including licensing procedures. Bus and truck drivers must adhere to the Motor Vehicle Safety Act of 1986. If you, for example, drive a vehicle with 16 or more passengers, you must have a Commercial Driver's License (CDL). A truck driver who drives a truck with a 26,000-pound capacity also has to have a CDL.

Generally speaking, drivers have to be at least 21 years old and in good physical condition, including hearing and vision. You can make a good living as a long-distance truck driver if you are willing to drive at night, work alone for long stretches at a time, and know the rules of the road.

Bus drivers usually receive from two to eight weeks' training where they learn rules and regulations, fare structure, and how to read schedules. They also get hands-on training driving the bus, including how to deal courteously with passengers. Since pay and benefits vary widely from city to city and company to company, you should check these out on an individual basis.

Railroad Workers

You may also decide to work for a railroad if you are interested in transportation. You wouldn't be alone: more than 300,000 people work for the railroads in this country. Trains transport people and freight, just as airplanes do, and specific jobs are available on the railroads: engineers, switchers, yard masters, brake operators, conductors, and train dispatchers.

Engineers run the trains, check them before and after the trip, monitor all the gauges during the trip, and keep in radio contact with traffic control centers about stops, starts, or delays.

Switchers operate the switches that move trains from track to track, keeping in radio contact with the yard engineer. Switchers can become yard masters, monitoring panels and activating switches and lights. Brake operators are part of the crew on freight trains. They inspect the train and make sure that it is on the right track. Passenger conductors will collect tickets, assist passengers, and see to the safety of passengers in an emergency. Dispatchers keep track of the movement of the trains, monitor the display panel, and transmit information to the engineer by radio.

It is rare for engineers, conductors, and brake operators to have regular hours. Their names go on an assignment board and when they reach their designated number of miles, the next person on the board takes the run. Those with little seniority are on 24-hour call.

You can get on-the-job training as a railroad worker. To become an engineer, you must be at least 21, have a high school diploma or equivalent, be in good physical condition, and complete the training course. Sometimes you can become an engineer after being a brake operator.

Your salary will vary from company to company, but you must be certified and licensed by the Federal Railroad Administration. However, you should keep in mind that this job, as well as that of bus driver and flight attendant, was recently listed by the National Institute for Safety and Health as a high-stress profession.

Driving a Cab

All jobs that deal with the public are generally considered to be high-stress positions, including driving a cab. And although you don't need any special education to be a driver, your communication skills in English; your knowledge of the city you are driving in, along with your map-reading skills; your ability to get along with a great variety of people, sometimes from all over the world; and, of course, your excellent driving skills all combine to make you a good cab driver.

You will also have to go through a brief training period, pass a written test, and have a valid chauffeur's license. Since cabs run 24 hours a day, 365 days a year in all weather conditions, you may get the graveyard shift if you are a true night owl.

Many cities issue guidelines for consumers so they know what to expect from cab companies and drivers. The Department of Consumer Services in Chicago, for example, issues a brochure called "How to use a Chicago Taxicab," which reminds passengers to accept rides from licensed cabs only, where the drivers are allowed to go, and what you should expect as far as fares are concerned.

The brochure also cautions the consumer to note license numbers, pictures of the cab driver that are prominently displayed, and the "medallion number." These identifications are important in case you leave something in the cab or have a complaint about the driver. And although there are always a million "cab driver" stories in any big city, we simply can't get along without them!

Profile of a Cab Driver

Rick Springer has been a cab driver for Flash Cab Co. in Chicago for the past 2-1/2 years. He knows about the stresses and real fears related to the job. For six years before he started driving, he was an inside salesperson both for machine tools for heavy industry and for veterinary medicine.

When the economy began to sag, he was laid off his job and was out of work for about 1-1/2 years. He worked part time as a carpet cleaner until the company lost its biggest account, and that was the end of that. At that point, Rick was 55 years old with very few marketable skills. But his back was up against a very hard wall, and he had to make some difficult decisions.

One of his friends, who had been a cab driver for several years, urged him to get his chauffeur's license and become a cab driver. As much as he needed a job, Rick didn't want anything to do with driving a cab—because he hated cab drivers. He thought they were terrible drivers, had bad attitudes toward other drivers, and didn't know their way around the city. He also had some fears about being robbed or shot as a cab driver in a big city.

As a longtime resident of Chicago, however, Rick felt that he really knew his way around, and he also knew he was a very good driver. Since he had, at one point in his life, delivered pizzas at night, he knew how to make a living with his driving skills. Still, he had his doubts, mainly because nighttime drivers are very vulnerable to robbery or worse.

But his money was dwindling and his friend kept pushing, and Rick decided to pay the $25 application fee for classes to earn a chauffeur's license. Along with the $25, he had to have a valid driver's license and be free and clear of traffic tickets.

He then took a three-day course that covered a lot of ground. Rick had to learn where hospitals, hotels, police stations, major tourist attractions, universities, and sports facilities are located. He had to study street guides and maps of the city; he had to know about the best routes to get from here to there; and he had to know the rules of the road and the laws pertaining to driving a cab. These included regulations for limiting the number of passengers allowed in the cab, jumping in front of other cabs in a pickup line, and picking up all passengers regardless of appearance or destination.

Oral communications were tested in class, and a written test was given at the end of the course. Although you don't have to fulfill any educational requirements to drive a cab, you do have to be able to communicate in English.

Rick passed the test the first time and then had to interview with a cab company—even though he still didn't want to be a cab driver. Again, his friend pushed him to interview with Flash Cab. He did, but he failed an oral test that was a major part of the interview. Rick went back to the books and passed the next time. He finally took the plunge and decided to take the night shift, even though he still had some doubts about his decision.

He was still worried about security, but he was also afraid that his first passenger would want to go to some exotic location that he had never heard of. He was afraid that he wouldn't know the best routes and that he would disappoint his customer.

With a little time, though, Rick began to have fun on the job. He works four nights a week: Monday, Wednesday, Friday, and Saturday. On week nights, he works from 5 P.M. to about 1:30 A.M. On weekends, he works from 5 P.M. to 5 A.M., when the bars close. For most of his life, Rick was a "day" person, working from 9 to 5. The adjustment took a few months, but now he is almost addicted to the job and the hours.

Rick loves the independence of the job, knowing that he can stop and start when he wants. He also loves to drive and meet people from all over the world and has gained new appreciation for the beauty and cleanliness of Chicago from his passengers.

Another bonus for him is that he earns his pay in cash directly and immediately. But because of this, he has to keep exact tax records because no deductions are taken from his pay.

7. Are you able to laugh at yourself if you've made a mistake and learn from it?

8. Are you a responsible driver or do you have a lot of tickets for speeding?

9. Can you communicate well with other people? In English? In any other language?

10. Can you do a job or complete a project without being constantly supervised?

If you answered questions 1 to 4 and 7, 9, and 10 positively, you are probably well suited to transportation work. If, for question 5 you said you were responsible; for question 6, independent; and for question 8, responsible, you're well on your way to a career in some phase of transportation. Now you just have to find your niche and pursue your goal.

For Further Information

Air Transport Association of America
1709 New York Ave., NW
Washington, DC 20006

Air Line Pilots Association
1625 Massachusetts Ave., NW
Washington, DC 20036

American Bus Association
1015 15th St., NW
Suite 250
Washington, DC 20005

American Public Transit Association
1201 New York Ave., NW
Suite 400
Washington, DC 20005

American Trucking Associations
2200 Mill Rd.
Alexandria, VA 22314-4677

Association of American Railroads
50 F St., NW
Washington, DC 20001

Brotherhood of Locomotive Engineers
Standard Building
Cleveland, OH 44113-1702

Future Aviation Professionals of America
4291 S. Memorial Dr.
Atlanta, GA 30032

Maritime Administration
U.S. Department of Transportation
400 7th St., SW
Washington, DC 20590

National Highway Traffic Safety Administration
U.S. Department of Transportation
NTS-22
400 7th St., SW
Washington, DC 20590

Professional Truck Driver Institute of America
8788 Elk Grove Blvd.
Suite M
Elk Grove, CA 95624

Publications

Air Traffic Control: How to Become an FAA Air Traffic Controller. Random House Reference, Mail Service Dept. ATC, 201 East 50th St., New York, NY 10022.

Air Traffic Control Specialists. Brief 322, Chronicle Guidance Publications, Inc., Aurora St., Moravia, NY 13118.

Airline Pilot Career Information. Air Line Pilots Association, 1625 Massachusetts Ave., NW, Washington, DC 20036.

Airline Pilots, Commercial, Brief 29. Chronicle Guidance Publications, Inc., Aurora St., Moravia, NY 13118.

Bus Drivers, Brief 52. Chronicle Guidance Publications, Inc., Aurora St., Moravia, NY 13118.

Career Options in Air Traffic Control & Airway Facilities. Air Traffic Control Association, Inc., 2300 Clarendon Blvd., Suite 711, Arlington, VA 22201.

Careers in Truck Driving. Office of Public Affairs, American Trucking Associations, 2200 Mill Rd., Alexandria, VA 22314.

List of Certified Pilot Schools. Superintendent of Documents, U.S. Government Printing Office, Washington, DC, 20402.

The People of the Airlines. Air Transport Association, Suite 1100, 1301 Pennsylvania Ave., NW, Washington, DC 20004-1707.

Railroad Industry Workers. Brief 14, Chronicle Guidance Publications, Inc., Aurora St., Moravia, NY 13118.

This is the FAA. U.S. Department of Transportation, Federal Aviation Administration, 800 Independence Ave., SW, Washington, DC 20591.

What to Look for in a Truck Driver Training School. Office of Public Affairs, American Trucking Associations, 2200 Mill Rd., Alexandria, VA 22314-4677.

Your Career in Aviation: The Sky's the Limit. U.S. Department of Transportation, Federal Aviation Administration, 800 Independence Ave., SW, Washington, DC 20591.

CHAPTER THREE

The Hospitality Industry

The word "hospitality" conjures all sorts of pleasant images—a clean room, comfortable bed, delicious food and drink, room service, congenial employees, chocolates on the pillow of the turned-down bed, soaps and shampoos in the bathroom ready for our use, and the luxury of having breakfast in bed.

Hospitality also means people who help us with our luggage and arrange for tickets and restaurant reservations. It involves still others who know how to direct us around a new town to see the best sights or get to our business meeting.

These are the people in the hotel, motel, and restaurant field, better known as the hospitality industry. The one thing all these people have in common is the goal of pleasing the customer, or in hospitality terms, serving the guest. Whether you decide to be a bellhop or the manager of a huge hotel, serving the guest is your primary goal.

What is it like to be a part of this growing field? It involves many opportunities for advancement because it employs so many people in such a wide variety of jobs.

Currently, the hotel/motel industry claims 1.64 million full-time and part-time workers. In the last 10 years, the travel industry has increased by 43 percent, and by the year 2000, the lodging industry probably will increase by 25 percent. In all, there are more than 3 million hotel rooms in this country that have to be serviced 365 days a year, 24 hours a day, including weekends and holidays. So, if you are a night owl, there is a place for you in this industry. You just have to decide which job you'd like the most.

Because this is a worldwide industry, your job possibilities are truly global. Even if you work in the United States, you will meet people from all over the world. Each day can be a new adventure because each day may bring new guests from any-where in the world whose needs must be met. The skills you learn in the United States can also be easily transferred to ho-tels and restaurants in other countries, too. International op-portunities are open to you, therefore, if you choose hospital-ity for your career.

Hospitality Careers for Night Owls

Let's take a look at some of the jobs available in hotels and motels. You could become a front-desk clerk, reservationist, concierge, rooms division manager, food and beverage director, host, maître d'hotel, chef, wine steward, busperson, food server, baker, bartender, executive housekeeper, room attendant, bell captain, security director, or door attendant. You could work your way up to assistant general manager and finally manager. And this is just a partial list of possible jobs for you to explore.

Getting Started

How do you get started? There are several ways to begin a ca-reer in hotels and motels. Since hours are flexible, you may be able to get a part-time job with a hotel while you are still in high school or college. Some high schools and many junior colleges, four-year colleges, and universities now offer courses in hotel management, which provide an excellent way to break into the field. Although it is still possible to start at the bottom of the ladder and work your way up to top management, more and more hotels and motels are requiring degrees and specialized training in order to advance. The more training and education you receive along the way, the more valuable you are to the organization.

The industry does, however, pride itself in providing thorough on-the-job training and promotion from within. Many businesses offer opportunities for continuing education and flexible hours. Since so many jobs operate on a 21-shift week instead of the normal five, schedules can often be arranged to comply with the needs of mothers, students, or senior citizens.

If you work for a hotel or motel chain, one of the benefits of employment is that you may be able to relocate to other cities in this country or in the world. Competitive salaries, life insurance, savings plans, and health insurance are standard benefits in most hotels. Some also provide free meals, laundry or dry cleaning, paid vacations, and training programs.

The Hotel Industry

Now let's go back and take a look at some of the jobs in a hotel or motel and examine some of the responsibilities. If you have a lot of patience and want to be of help to everyone who stays at the hotel, you may want to consider the front-desk position. These employees check guests in and out, assign rooms, assist guests in finding their way around town, and often help the concierge in making reservations. They must be able to answer questions about the hotel and its services, the time it takes to get to the airport, shopping opportunities, and the best sights and restaurants in town.

These clerks have to be flexible, courteous, and patient because their personality and knowledge will be extremely important in ensuring that the guest will have a pleasant stay and perhaps be a guaranteed return. Some of the larger hotels and motels may have as many as 1,000 check-ins and checkouts in a day, so this is really a public relations position.

In 1990, approximately 118,000 people were employed as front-desk clerks and there are good prospects for employment into the next century. Since international travel is expected to grow along with business travel, people who know a foreign language may be in greater demand in the future. Jobs may also open up because there is rather high turnover in this position and because the hours are flexible.

Food Service

Maybe you'd rather work in the kitchen as a cook or a chef. To a certain extent, both titles imply that the employees do the same thing: follow recipes, know about kitchen equipment, and arrange the food in an appetizing way.

The chef, however, is the most highly trained kitchen worker, often known for specially created dishes prepared and presented in an innovative way. Chefs plan restaurant and banquet menus and supervise other kitchen staff. Some hotels have coffee shops and fast-food restaurants that employ cooks who prepare much more limited fare. Kitchen workers in hotels are subject to late shifts, holiday work, and weekend hours.

Education and Training

You can start out as a short-order cook without a high school education and receive on-the-job training. However, in order to become a chef, you will need years of training and experience. You will have to undergo an apprenticeship program in a professional setting, such as a culinary institute, trade union, professional association, or college. The larger hotels may also offer training programs. Some training facilities include courses in supervision and management.

You will learn how to bake, broil, sauté, and grill food; plan menus; purchase and store foods; and keep sanitary conditions in the kitchen. When you complete your training, which may last up to two years, you will want to be certified by the American Culinary Foundation. This group sets the standards for the industry and assures the quality of your training.

You may be in the position to supervise other employees on the job. You could then be promoted to executive chef or kitchen, dining room, or restaurant manager. At any rate, your job prospects look very favorable in the future because of projected growth in the hospitality industry.

The National Restaurant Association provides two possible scenarios for advancing in the restaurant business. In the first, you would start off as an assistant cook and work up to cook and then to chef. From there you could become assistant manager and then manager. Another route would be to start out as a busperson, become a waiter, then a host, assistant manager, and finally manager. Other entry-level positions that can lead you up the ladder are cashier, baker, or kitchen assistant. With some experience and training, you might become a dining room manager, pastry chef, or bartender. From there you might become an executive chef, menu planner, dietitian, or food-service manager.

The host at a restaurant greets the customers at the door, maintains the reservations list, and escorts guests to their tables. A pleasant personality and good organizational skills are necessary for this position.

The kitchen assistant helps the cooks, chefs, and bakers in the mixing and preparation of ingredients. Buspersons clear the tables after the guests have left and set the tables for the next customers. During the course of the meal, they refill water glasses and coffee cups. They also may help the waiters with other housekeeping duties.

Waiters and bartenders are needed nights, weekends, and holidays in hotel restaurants. Waiters take orders, serve food and beverages, and prepare bills for customers. Depending on the restaurant, they may recommend wines and beverages, describe food preparation, and even prepare special dishes at the table. During the course of the meal, they check on the customers to see whether they need anything and whether everything is satisfactory. Additional duties, such as escorting the customers to their tables or cleaning the tables and serving areas, may also be required.

Bartenders prepare drinks for the customers and often socialize with them. They must know how to mix drinks, order liquor and supplies, keep the bar attractive, wash glasses as needed, and prepare fruit and other drink condiments.

There are no real educational requirements for waiters and bartenders, although bartenders can take courses at bartending schools. On-the-job training usually suffices for either job. What is important for these jobs is a pleasant personality, a good memory, and patience. Since both jobs have a lot of public contact, you have to like working with people and want to serve them efficiently.

Most waiters and bartenders work for a basic hourly wage plus tips. Therefore, the base pay may not be much more than about $5 an hour to start. You may, after some time, earn up to $9 an hour; those working in very elegant restaurants will earn higher wages. If you do well, you might become a supervisor or work in banquet services or as dining-room manager.

If you aspire to higher levels in the restaurant business, you may become the food-service manager, who is responsible for setting quality, efficiency, and profitability standards for the restaurant. The food production manager supervises the kitchen staff and sets costs and standards for sanitation.

The executive chef supervises all sous-chefs, or under-chefs, and cooks and is responsible for the menu. This position requires specific training, apprenticeship, and certification. The menu planner works closely with the executive chef and usually has to have a bachelor's or associate's degree.

Earnings

The food-service industry truly does offer jobs for people of all education and training levels and rewards them according to merit, enthusiasm, creativity, and willingness to serve. However, if you work for tips, your base pay may be comparatively small.

The 1988 hourly median wages before tips for a bartender were $4.75; for a waiter, $2.35; for a host, $4.75, and for a busperson, $3.50. These figures may not be representative of the entire industry, but may serve as a guideline. Workers who earn tips may be paid less than minimum wage as a base rate, providing the opportunity exists to reach or exceed minimum wage with tips.

It's estimated by the National Restaurant Association that tips could raise your income by $20,000-$30,000 a year. Uniforms and meals may also be supplied by the restaurant. Even though restaurants require shift work, it may work to your advantage. Students, housewives, aspiring actors, and musicians have found working in restaurants a satisfying way to make a living, to meet interesting people, to receive valuable on-the-job training, and to work up the ladder if they choose.

Housekeeping

No matter how long we stay in a hotel, probably the most important element in our comfort is our room. All the great food in the world can't make up for a room that is not clean or well maintained. We love those clean sheets and towels; shampoo, soaps, and tissues in the bathroom; newly vacuumed carpets;

and polished furniture and mirrors. We like to think that no one else has ever been there before us.

For all this cleanliness and comfort, we have the housekeeping staff to thank.

In hotels, housekeeping is always one of the largest departments—in larger hotels, there may be several hundred employees. Both staff members and executives usually work longer hours during tourist season, when everybody may be on call.

The room attendants, laundry personnel, linen-room workers, and floor supervisors are all part of that staff. The executive housekeeper oversees their work. It has been customary for this position to be filled by a senior staff member. However, there are now college courses and certification programs that prepare you for this management position.

Education and Training

The National Executive Housekeeper Association (NEHA) is the professional association which offers a 330-hour training and certification program for those who aspire to this position. The executive housekeeper prepares budgets, trains staff, solves personnel problems, and oversees inventory of supplies.

Room attendants and laundry personnel generally do not need specific education or training. Most learn their skills on the job. However, to advance to an executive position, you will need to have specific education, training, and skills. The NEHA recommends college courses in sociology, psychology, economics, communications, and budgeting. Accounting and computer classes are always helpful. You will need good organizational, communications, and motivational skills.

Job prospects are good, especially if you have education and experience. Since the executive housekeeper position is at the top of the housekeeping department, you could advance to become assistant manager and then general manager.

Hotel Management

The top position in most hotels and motels is the general manager. These managers are in charge of the overall operation of the hotel, including preparing the budget, setting quality standards for all departments, and following the policies of the owner or hotel chain executive. Many of the larger hotels have assistant general managers for each of the various departments.

Like other employees of the lodging industry, the managers work irregular hours—evenings, nights, weekends, and holidays, with particularly long hours during conventions or peak tourist seasons. Managers can work for a corporation or own their own establishments.

Education and Training

As in all other hotel positions, training and education are important because the industry is becoming more and more professional. Managers, in particular, must have college degrees. A liberal arts degree is acceptable if you also have some hotel or restaurant management experience.

However, you can now get a bachelor's degree in hotel management. Courses include accounting, marketing, housekeeping, and data processing. If you can get a job in a hotel during your summer breaks or after school in conjunction with your degree, you have a better chance at landing a managerial position.

It still is possible, in some hotels, to get on-the-job training by working in every department until you learn all aspects of the hotel's operations. You also may be required to relocate to other hotels or motels in the chain. Certification, including course work, from the American Hotel and Motel Association (AH&MA) can land you a management position in conjunction with this training.

Earnings

Along with other jobs in the lodging industry, managerial positions will continue to grow. Recent salary ranges record an average annual salary for managers as $56,000, depending on the size of the facility. Benefits are good, and bonuses are also possible.

You and your family may also enjoy free lodging, meals, laundry, and other perks of the job. You will probably also receive standard medical and life insurance, as well as a pension plan. So, if you want to get into a line of work where the customer is always right, some aspect of the hospitality industry may be right for you.

Profile of a Former Hotel Manager

Dean Kelley, who is now the Oil and Gas Property Manager at Continental Bank in Chicago, indirectly got this job because of his background in the hotel business. He served first as concierge for the bank, after many years working for various hotels and motels—and that included working nights and being on call 24 hours a day.

When Dean was a sophomore in college, he worked part time at a local hotel. This job included maintenance and repair work, with hours from either 3 to 11 P.M. or 4 P.M. to midnight. He was working on his B.A. in business, but there were no hospitality courses offered at that time. He was at a point in his life, though, where he was wondering what he was going to do for a living.

The hotel business seemed to offer good opportunities for quick advancement and good salaries. So, with a combination of his experience at the hotel and his college education, he thought he could rapidly become an assistant manager of a small property.

That's exactly what happened. After graduating from college, he became assistant manager for a Red Roof Inn in Grand Rapids, Michigan. He started out learning how to work the night audit, which included front-desk work and balancing the books.

After that, he went to Atlanta, Georgia, to the company's general manager training school, where he learned operational procedures relating to the financial running of the hotel. After this internship period, Dean was transferred to Cincinnati, Ohio, where he became an assistant manager.

He was promoted to manager within a year, but in the meantime, Dean had to oversee the front-desk, maintenance, and housekeeping staffs. He hired and trained them and handled all personnel problems. Meanwhile he was also learning more about the financial aspects of running the hotel from his manager. Dean was working all shifts at this time: 9 to 5, 3 to 11, or 11 to 7, with emphasis on the heaviest check-in and checkout times.

Dean worked as assistant manager for about a year and was then promoted to general manager in Dayton, Ohio. After a year, he was hired by Marriott as a sales manager. As such, he had to try to find clients who were going to stay at the hotel for more than one night, preferably at least a week or even a month. This job involved making cold calls, researching corporations, and networking with companies to see if he could get their business. In the process, Dean did a lot of wining and dining of prospective clients. He enjoyed the work and continued it for about a year.

But Dean decided that he wanted to go back to hotel management and was promoted to a general manager position in Ann Arbor, Michigan. He remained in that position for about two years and was then hired by the Hyatt Regency in Chicago as an assistant manager.

This 2,000-room hotel was the largest he had managed so far. There were actually three assistant managers who rotated schedules on a monthly basis. At the time, Dean thought that the 11 P.M. to 7 A.M. shift was difficult, but interesting. Much of his work involved monitoring other employees to make sure they weren't sleeping in one of the many hiding places that such a large hotel would have. As you might guess, Dean has a million stories to tell about hotels at night and what goes on in the dark!

But this shift played havoc with Dean's sleeping habits. Not a born night owl, he was always tired when he got home and just wanted to sleep. Dean says, however, that sleeping during the day is not the same as sleeping at night. He never got a restful sleep during those hours because it was never dark enough to block out the sun.

He also was distracted by the noises of the street traffic. And when he got up at about 5 P.M., he wanted to run errands, but he couldn't go to the bank or to certain stores because they were closed. His eating habits suffered on this shift, and he had virtually no social life. Dean was glad that this shift only lasted a year.

At this time, Dean again took a look at his future prospects. In retrospect, he had done very well and moved up the ranks quickly. But he was also considering the fact that he never got vacations, did not have a social life, and was always on call. At that point, he decided that he was probably not a night owl, and the hotel business was not what he wanted to do forever. He took the 9-to-5 job at the bank. He was able to successfully transfer many of the skills he had acquired in the hotel business to a new line of work, but one where he could finally get a good night's sleep.

Dean does think, however, that the hotel industry has many advantages for the right person. You can, with hard work, advance rather quickly and receive very good on-the-job training. You may have to relocate in order to advance, and you will definitely have to work different shifts.

Is the Hospitality Industry for You?

If you decide to work for a hotel, you should be computer literate, have good communication and math skills, and be patient. You should also develop a sense of humor, if you don't already have one. You will have to assume a great deal of responsibility and learn to do many things, but you can make a very good living in hotels—if you can just learn to sleep during the day!

For those of you who may still be considering a career in the hospitality industry, you may now want to take a look at what the industry is all about, what you might contribute to it, and what it may offer you. The word "hospitality" just about says it all: It means quality service to the guest, including comfort, courtesy, security, grace under pressure, personality, skill, reliability, and style.

It also means that the customer is always right. And that means that you are there to see to it that the customer is satisfied with the room, the food, the cleanliness, the competence, and the friendliness.

There is a special mind set in this industry, and it has to do with putting yourself in someone else's shoes. If you work in a hotel, for example, you have to imagine how tired and hassled travelers might be and how you can help to relieve the stress of being in a strange city in an unfamiliar setting. They might be there on business or for pleasure, but it is still sometimes stressful to get settled comfortably in new surroundings. Whether a guest is alone, a member of a business team, or with family or friends, he or she will need to be guided by the skillful hands of professional hotel personnel.

Travelers also expect a room with clean linens, air conditioning, color television, extra blankets, and—in more luxurious accommodations—a chocolate on the pillow. Experts in housekeeping see to it that weary travelers have all the supplies they need to have a comfortable stay at the hotel.

Many people who travel do so because they want to try new food experiences in new settings prepared in innovative ways. They may be tired of tuna sandwiches, burgers, and fries. They are looking for something special, and they will find it either in the restaurant of the hotel or somewhere in the destination city.

Therefore, the chefs, waiters, and hosts are there to make sure that breakfast, lunch, and dinner are served on time, are presented with style, and, above all, taste good.

What It Takes

In other words, if you decide to make a career in the hospitality industry, you need certain personal qualities, as well as skills and training. You definitely want to have a feel for people's needs, especially when they might be under the stress of being in unfamiliar territory.

You must to be able to adapt to people who have special needs, such as those who are in wheelchairs or who have special dietary needs. In addition, you need to understand people who are in a party mood and are looking for fun when you are dead on your feet and just want to go home to sleep. Your pleasant personality and your ability to meet the needs of the customer are all-important in the hospitality industry.

Now is the time to measure your "hospitality index." Do you think you can put on a smiling face, meet the various needs of your customers, and make sure they are satisfied? Are you developing these skills now in your personal life? Are you working weekends or summers as a waiter or bellhop to find out what hospitality is all about?

Are you an outgoing person who looks after people at parties to see whether they are enjoying themselves? Do you see to it that they have enough to eat and drink? Do you make sure that they are comfortable and enjoying themselves?

If you have these qualities, you are a prime candidate for the hospitality industry. There may be a career for you there, especially if you are a night owl.

Answer the following questions to see whether you are suited to hotel work.

1. Do you actively participate in the preparation of parties or special events in your home when guests are coming?

2. Do you like to cook or experiment with recipes?

3. Are you aware of what is going on in your community as far as concerts, special events, guest appearances, sporting events, or personal appearances are concerned?

4. Do you have a knack for making people comfortable, even in an unfamiliar environment?

5 Are you reliable, dependable, and eager to please?

If you can answer most of these questions positively, you are probably suited to a career in the hospitality industry.

For Further Information

Organizations

American Culinary Federation
P.O. Box 3466
St. Augustine, FL 32085

American Hotel & Motel Association
1201 New York Ave., NW
Washington, DC 20005-3931

American Hotel Foundation
610 South Belardo Rd.
Suite 650
Palm Springs, CA 92264

American Institute of Wine and Food
1550 Bryant St.
San Francisco, CA 94103

Careers, Inc.
P.O. Box 135
Largo, FL 34294-0135

Council on Hotel, Restaurant and Institutional Education
(CHRIE)
1200 17th St., NW
7th Floor
Washington, DC 20036-3097

Educational Foundation of the National Restaurant Association
250 South Wacker Dr.
Suite 1400
Chicago, IL 60606

The Educational Institute of American Hotel & Motel Association
P.O. Box 1240
East Lansing, MI 48826

Hospitality Sales & Marketing Association International
1300 L St., NW
Suite 800
Washington, DC 20005

International Foodservice Executives Association
1100 South State Rd., #7
Suite 103
Margate, FL 33068

National Association of Catering Executives
2500 Wilshire Blvd.
Suite 603
Los Angeles, CA 90057

National Association of Trade and Technical Schools
P.O. Box 10429
Department BL
Rockville, MD 20850

National Executive Housekeepers Association
1001 Eastwind Dr.
Suite 301
Westerville, OH 43081-3361

Periodicals and Books

Beverage World. 150 Great Neck Rd., Great Neck, NY 11021 (monthly).
Brief 358: Executive Housekeepers (Directors of Housekeeping). Chronicle
 Guidance Publications, Inc. P.O. Box 1190, Moravia, NY 13118.
Cooking for Profit. CP Publishing, 104 South Main St., #717, Fond du
 Lac, WI 54935 (monthly).
Cornell Hotel & Restaurant Administration Quarterly. Statler Hall, Cornell
 University, Ithaca, NY 14853 (bimonthly).
Executive Housekeeper. Educational Research Council of America,
 Changing Times Education Service, 300 York Ave., St. Paul, MN
 55101.
Executive Housekeeping Today. National Executive Housekeepers Associa-
 tion, Inc., 1001 Eastwind Dr., Suite 301, Westerville, OH 43081-3361
 (monthly).
From Check-In to Check-Out. Education Institute of the American Hotel
 & Motel Association. P.O. Box 1240, East Lansing, MI 48826-1240
 (video).

The Guide to Hospitality and Tourism Education—A Directory of CHRIE Member Colleges and Universities. Council on Hotel, Restaurant and Institutional Education, 1200 17th St., NW, 7th Floor, Washington, DC 20036-3097.

Hospitality: A World of Opportunities. Education Institute of the American Hotel & Motel Association, P.O. Box 1240, East Lansing, MI 48826-1240 (video).

Hospitality Design. Bill Communications, 355 Park Ave. South, New York, NY 10010 (10 issues).

Hosteur. Council of Hotel, Restaurant, and Institutional Education, 1200 17th St., NW, Washington, DC 20036-3097 (semiannual).

Hotels. Cahners Publishing Co., Subscription Office, 44 Cook St., Denver, CO 80206 (monthly).

Managing Bar and Beverage Operations. Education Institute of the American Hotel & Motel Association, P.O. Box 1240, East Lansing, MI 48826-1240.

Managing Front Office Operations. Education Institute of the American Hotel & Motel Association, P.O. Box 1240, East Lansing, MI 48826-1240.

Managing Housekeeping Operations. Education Institute of the American Hotel & Motel Association, P.O. Box 1240, East Lansing, MI 48826-1240.

Managing Human Resources in the Hospitality Industry. Education Institute of the American Hotel & Motel Association, P.O. Box 1240, East Lansing, MI 48826-1240.

Model Position Descriptions. Council on Hotel, Restaurant and Institutional Education, 1200 17th St., NW, Washington, DC 20036-3097.

Nightclub & Bar. Oxford Publishing, 305 West Jackson Ave., Oxford, MS 38655 (monthly).

Professional Dining Room Service. Education Institute of the American Hotel & Motel Association, P.O. Box 1240, East Lansing, MI 48826-1240 (two videos).

Restaurant Business. Bill Communications, 355 Park Ave. South, New York, NY 10010 (18 issues/year).

Restaurant Hospitality. Penton Publications, 1100 Superior Ave., Cleveland, OH 44114 (monthly).

Restaurant Management Insider, Walker Communications, Inc., 1541 Morris Ave., Bronx, NY 10457 (monthly).

Restaurants & Institutions, Cahners Publishing Co., Subscription Office, 44 Cook St., Denver, CO 80206 (biweekly).

Restaurants USA, National Restaurant Association, 1200 17th St., NW, Washington, DC 20036 (monthly).

Training for the Hospitality Industry, Education Institute of the American Hotel & Motel Association, P.O. Box 1240, East Lansing, MI 48826-1240.

CHAPTER FOUR

The Health Care Industry

All of us know how important good health is and how we rely on health care providers to be there whenever we need them. This is one career group that has always had to be on call day and night—to perform emergency surgery, to deliver babies, to heal wounds, to monitor patients' progress, to administer medicine, and to advise and comfort the loved ones of the patient.

Human health needs—from the cradle to the grave—occur and are taken care of at all times of day or night by a wide range of professionals who have specific responsibilities. However, the first specialist we may think of when we are sick or injured is the doctor.

Doctors, in turn, rely on a number of medical personnel, including physician assistants, nurses, technicians, laboratory personnel, technologists, and emergency medical technicians. These are highly skilled professionals who must attain a certain level of education, training, and experience to qualify for health care work.

Physicians

Let's start with physicians, who diagnose and treat sickness and disease after conducting physical exams. They also work to prevent disease by advising patients about nutrition, life-style, and hygiene.

The physicians we will discuss are M.D.s, or doctors of medicine. Other physicians practice as D.O.s, or doctors of osteopathy. D.O.s diagnose and recommend therapy based on the premise that bone structure must be aligned for proper health.

Physicians usually specialize in a specific part or region of the body or in a type of disease. For example, physicians can specialize in heart disease, pediatrics, internal medicine, skin disease, oncology, neurology, obstetrics, urology, or otolaryngology. Or they may perform neurological, gynecological, plastic, thoracic, or general surgery.

Physicians work in clinics, hospitals, offices, health maintenance organizations (HMOs), and for the military—sometimes even in combat zones. If health reform occurs in this country, still other possibilities may open up to physicians and other health care providers. All in all, about 600,000 physicians practice in the United States. They find jobs in large cities, suburbs, small towns, and rural communities.

If you work anywhere in the United States as an M.D., you will have to be licensed. This means that you must be a graduate of an accredited medical school, pass a licensing exam, and serve a residency for one to six years. You most likely will need a bachelor's degree from a four-year college or university to get into medical school.

While in college or at the university, be sure to study science courses, including biology, chemistry, biochemistry, anatomy, and physics. Also include in your course work communications skills, math, and social sciences. Knowledge of computers is also becoming necessary for health care work.

In order to get into medical school, you will have to pass the Medical College Admission Test (MCAT). If you are admitted to medical school (the competition is keen), your course work will include physiology, microbiology, anatomy, and pathology.

You will learn to observe patients in hospitals and will work with children, expectant mothers, people with serious injuries, or those with emotional problems. You will also begin to learn how to diagnose and treat illnesses.

After you have successfully completed medical school, you must pass an exam given by the National Board of Medical Examiners to become a resident. After your residency, you will have to be board certified by passing a test administered by the American Board of Medical Specialists.

There are 24 areas in which you can be board certified:

1. Allergy and immunology

2. Anesthesiology

3. Colon and rectal surgery

4. Dermatology

5. Emergency medicine

6. Family practice

7. Internal medicine

8. Neurological surgery

9. Neurology

10. Nuclear medicine

11. Obstetrics and gynecology

12. Ophthalmology

13. Orthopedic surgery

14. Otolaryngology

15. Pathology

16. Pediatrics

17. Physical medicine and rehabilitation

18. Plastic surgery

19. Preventative medicine

20. Psychiatry

21. Radiology

22. Surgery

23. Thoracic surgery

24. Urology

If you decide to teach in any one of these specialties or want to conduct research in them, you will probably need further study and academic degrees. From the time you are a resident and often long after, you may need to work split shifts, graveyard shifts, or even 24-hour shifts.

What It Takes

What are some qualities that you will need to become a physician? You will definitely want to be able to help people, be willing to work under stress, be able to work well individually and as a member of a team, and make decisions quickly if there is an emergency situation.

If you are still in high school, be sure to take a broad base of courses, including English, computers, biology, chemistry, physics, and math. Your extracurricular activities in both high school and college may prove to be important in getting into medical school, where well-rounded personalities are considered valuable.

Since you will, as a physician, often have to make life-and-death decisions, you should start early in your life establishing priorities, gathering information, making decisions, and following through. You may also want to determine how well you respond in emergency situations. For instance, can you keep a level head when things go wrong? How do you react to a sick or injured person or animal? Do you have patience and understanding when people are suffering or in pain? Or do you faint at the sight of blood? How you answer these questions may help you to determine whether you should become a doctor.

The work load can also be grueling. During medical school, you will be studying long hours. As a resident, you may be working 24-hour shifts. And, depending on your specialty, you may be doing shift work or be on call for the rest of your working life. After all, who can tell when a baby will be born?

Earnings

And although your education is long and hard, the rewards, both professionally and financially, can be great. Physicians are among the best paid of all professionals, and job prospects look good for the immediate future. Recent salary estimates for physicians, depending on their specialties and where they work, range from $95,000 to $220,000 per year with an average annual salary of $155,000. Residents' salaries range from $26,000 to $33,000.

Many changes may take place in the health care system in the next few years that physicians and health care providers will have to take into account. Even with these changes, however, physicians will be needed at hospitals, in clinics, in private practice or HMOs, both in big cities and in rural settings. There may be a rise in the need for geriatric care because American citizens are aging. Primary care physicians will always be needed. As long as we all have so many parts that can and do go wrong, we will need doctors to repair them.

Emergency Medical Physicians

Night owls are definitely needed in this demanding area of medicine. Emergency medical physicians are always subject to shift work. According to a recent survey in *Emergency Medicine News*, the number one reason why physicians leave emergency medicine is shift work, although other factors may contribute to burnout.

Although emergency medicine is now an official specialty, it is a relatively new one—only 25 years old. Approximately 800 physicians graduate annually from the 101 emergency medicine residency programs in this country. Previously, however, many doctors who worked in emergency rooms were moonlighters whom no one took seriously.

Unfortunately, remnants of those old feelings remain today among nonemergency personnel. Emergency physicians also cite emotional and physical stress, family considerations, and work load pressures as reasons for leaving the emergency room.

Profile of an Emergency Physician

Rebecca Roberts grew up in a very small town in the state of Washington. In fact, the town was so small that the telephone book was only three pages long. Nobody in her family had chosen health care for a career. They were actually people who never went to a doctor except in cases of emergency. Her mother went to a doctor only once that Rebecca can remember. That was for a bleeding ulcer and only when it was too painful to ignore. She also remembers that her father went to see a doctor only when he'd had a heart attack. Rebecca herself only went to the doctor when she had to be immunized for school. So where did her desire to become a doctor come from?

She really wanted to do something that would help people. Rebecca was very good at science and math and wanted to utilize her strengths in her career. She also wanted something absorbing, and she thought medicine would fulfill that need.

When she was in her sophomore year at the University of Washington as a philosophy major, a professor reminded her that there were no jobs available for philosophy majors, except maybe in the law. She knew that she didn't want to spend her life arguing with other people, so that year, Rebecca switched majors and decided to go into medicine. Because she switched midstream, it took her five years to finish her undergraduate work instead of four. She had to take certain science courses, for example, that were not required for philosophy.

Then she had to attend four years of medical school and one year of internship. Rebecca had pretty much decided on family practice. She spent one year in urgent care medicine and took her residency at the University of Chicago. She got there as a result of the National Physicians' Matching Program, which is a rather complicated, but nearly flawless, computerized system that places residents in the hospitals of their choice.

In many programs today, the internship and residency are combined with three years of emergency room experience and an additional three years of study. After such a program, you would be board eligible in emergency medicine. To become board certified, you have to take both written and oral exams, sometimes six months to a year apart.

These exams are given at precisely the same time at different sites, such as Chicago, Dallas, Los Angeles, and New York. Security is very tight at these exams. For example, you will have to bring your driver's license and picture identification with you, and your signature will be compared. You will have three opportunities to pass this test, but it is very expensive, especially when you factor in transportation to and from the testing site.

Six months to a year later, you will have to take your oral board exams, which consist of seven cases and fake scenarios.

You will have 15 minutes for each case—not a long time to prove yourself, but necessary to pass the test.

Rebecca passed all these tests and is now a senior physician in emergency medicine at Cook County Hospital in Chicago. She also serves as associate residency director for training programs for residents in the emergency room. As such, she works 10 shifts per month and is also on call. And during the World Cup soccer games in Chicago in 1994, no one was allowed to turn off the beeper; in other words, everyone was on call because of the possibilities of injury or accident.

Shift work can be dangerous when you are dealing with life-and-death situations. Therefore, scheduling has to be done carefully in medicine, and Rebecca prepares herself for her work for every shift by getting up very early, working hard, and going to bed early whenever she has to work long shifts. She also allows time for catching up on sleep.

Even though Rebecca has many responsibilities, she seems to have fulfilled her early goals for choosing medicine as her life's work. She's a true night owl. Sleep deprivation and lack of a normal social life don't deter her from what she feels is important. After all, that is what being a night owl is all about, isn't it?

Physician Assistants

Physician assistants work with the physician or surgeon at odd hours of the day and night. It may surprise you that, in 1992, *Working Woman* magazine chose physician assistant as one of the top 25 hottest careers. But maybe you've never heard of physician assistants. That may be because the physician assistant or PA position was just created in the 1960s because of the lack of primary physicians. Today there are more than 22,000 working PAs in the United States.

The functions you perform as a PA vary from location to location, but you will always be working under the supervision of a physician. You may also serve as an assistant in surgery. Physician assistants are qualified to perform the following functions:

1. Take medical histories

2. Perform physical exams

3. Order laboratory tests

4. Diagnose illness

5. Determine treatment

6. Advise patients

7. Assist in surgery

8. Prescribe radiation

Education and Training

Right now, there are more than 55 accredited PA programs in the United States, often linked to two- or four-year colleges or universities. These programs must meet minimum standards for accreditation.

Most programs take 102 weeks to complete. You'll be in the classroom the first year and in a clinic, hospital, or doctor's office the second year. In the first year, your course work will include:

1. Anatomy

2. Physiology

3. Pharmacology

4. Microbiology

5. Biochemistry

6. Pathology

7. Clinical lab

8. Health promotion

9. Clinical medicine

10. Medical ethics

11. Radiology

12. Psychosocial course work

In the second year, your clinical rotation will include:

1. Family medicine

2. Internal medicine

3. Emergency medicine

4. Pediatrics

5. Geriatric medicine

6. Obstetrics/gynecology

7. Surgery

8. Orthopedics

9. Psychiatry

You should have at least two years of college before you are admitted to a PA program. It's also a good idea to have some health care experience. Almost 50 percent of the applicants to PA programs do have bachelor's degrees. When you are in college, study English, biology, humanities, social sciences, chemistry, math, and psychology.

After you have completed your course work, you will have to take a certifying exam given by the National Commission of Certification of Physician Assistants (NCCPA). When you pass the test, you will have the title of Physician Assistant-Certified (PA-C). In order to remain certified, you will have to complete 100 hours of certified medical education courses every two years and take a recertification exam every six years.

Like physicians, PAs work in hospitals, clinics, private practices of physicians, HMOs, and the military—in cities, suburbs, and rural areas. Also like physicians, PAs can specialize in the following:

1. Emergency medicine

2. Family practice

3. Geriatrics

4. Industrial/occupational medicine

5. Internal medicine

6. Internal medicine subspecialities

7. Obstetrics/gynecology

8. Orthopedics

9. Pediatrics

10. Pediatric subspecialties

11. Surgery

12. Surgery subspecialties

As mentioned previously, however, PAs always work under the supervision of at least one physician. They also work within the scope of their expertise and the laws of the individual state.

Every state except Mississippi, including the District of Columbia and Guam, has licensing regulations concerning the practice of physician assistants. These specialists will also be exposed to shift work if their supervising physician is involved with flexible working hours or is on call.

Earnings

Salaries for PAs are good. In 1992, the majority of PAs were earning between $30,000 and $65,000 a year. Some even earn more than $100,000, depending on location, specialty, and years of experience. The job prospects also look good: The U.S. Department of Labor predicts a 56.7 percent increase in jobs by the year 2000.

Information about financial aid, loans, and scholarships is available through the American Academy of Physician Attendants. They will also provide you with information about financial awards for minorities, as well as a list of state financial aid agencies and availability and location of PA programs. According to all indications, this is a "hot" career opportunity.

More traditional, perhaps, is the career of the nurse. When we think of doctors, we almost automatically think of nurses. And when doctors do shift work, nurses are right beside them.

Nurses

Nurses make sure that patients are comfortable, give them their medication, help physicians during treatments, and record symptoms and progress of patients. Nurses are found in hospitals, nursing homes, doctors' offices, private businesses, government agencies, cities and rural areas—wherever doctors are practicing medicine.

Nurses who work in hospitals, in private duty, for the armed forces, and in companies that run on a 24-hour basis will be required to do shift work. For example, they will have to work weekends, evenings, graveyard shift, and holidays.

Registered Nurses

Registered nurses have to graduate from an accredited program and pass a national licensing examination. If you choose to become a registered nurse, you will have three options for obtaining the qualifications you need:

1. Associate Degree in Nursing (A.D.N.)

2. Bachelor of Science Degree in Nursing (B.S.N.)

3. Diploma

The associate degree is a two-year program and is offered through community or junior colleges. The B.S.N. degree is offered at colleges and universities and takes four or five years to complete. The diploma is issued through two-year programs in hospitals. As with other professions, nurses with the bachelor's degree will advance more quickly into administrative or supervisory positions. You will also need the B.S.N. if you want to get a higher degree, conduct research, or teach.

As with other health care professions, education includes both classroom work and clinical training. Course work will include anatomy, physiology, microbiology, chemistry, psychology, and nursing. Then you will receive supervised training in specific areas in a hospital setting.

Most nurses do end up in hospitals, including the emergency room. But hospital nurses may also be found in the operating room, in the intensive care unit, or in oncology. They administer the health care procedures as outlined by the supervising physician or surgeon for individual patients.

Many patients in private care need round-the-clock care. Therefore, nurses in this situation will expect shift work or rotating hours. These nurses are hired by families or agencies to take care of patients in their own homes, in nursing homes, or in hospitals.

Licensed Practical/Vocational Nurses

Licensed practical/vocational nurses (LP/VN) work in the same places that physicians, physician assistants, and registered nurses work. They work under the supervision of the physician or registered nurse, and although their responsibilities may vary, the LP/VN is primarily responsible for:

1. Bathing and feeding patients

2. Taking blood pressure

3. Administering medications

4. Giving treatments

5. Helping with diagnostic procedures

6. Observing symptoms

It will take you from nine to 18 months to complete both your classroom courses and clinical training. You will learn nursing skills, anatomy, physiology, pharmacology, and medical-surgical nursing. You can complete this work at hospital-based schools, community colleges, and vocational centers. After you have successfully completed this program, you will have to pass a licensing exam to practice as an LP/VN.

There are about 500,000 to 600,000 working LP/VNs in the United States today, and career opportunities are good for the immediate future. You will have to be patient, flexible, reliable, and tactful to be an LP/VN. Your starting salary will range from approximately $12,000 to $16,000 annually. Further experience will bring that up to $22,000.

Occupational Health Nurses

Since many companies run on a 24-hour basis, occupational health nurses (OHN) are needed at work sites to ensure the health and safety of the employees. The larger the facility and the more dangerous the work, the more the OHN is needed, and they will be needed on every shift.

The occupational health nurse should ideally be considered an important member of the management team. The individual company will decide the scope of the health and safety needs, the health programs required, the budgetary needs of the programs, and number of nurses needed. Some factors used in the decision making process may include:

1. Size of the company

2. Primary health and safety hazards

3. Health and safety needs of the staff

If, for example, an industrial company has 300 employees, it should staff one OHN; however, three nurses would be required in an industrial setting with up to 1,000 employees. These nurses will then be able to provide counseling for substance abuse or programs for quitting smoking, losing weight, or staying fit. They can monitor high-risk employees, teach the staff about safety precautions, act as liaison with insurance companies, and give physical exams to the employees.

The American Association of Occupational Health Nurses (AAOHN) is the professional organization for OHNs that sets the standards of excellence in education and research. They recommend the B.S.N. for all OHNs today in order to preserve the professional standards of registered nurses in this country. They also monitor government regulations and pending legislation as they relate to OHNs and publish a monthly journal and newsletter, an annual report, and job openings for members.

The Emergency Nurses Association (ENA) is the membership organization that sets the professional educational and research standards for emergency nurses. The association provides continuing education programs, networking opportunities, a trauma nursing core course, an emergency nursing pediatric course, and various publications.

The ENA also encourages emergency nurses to attain the Certified Emergency Nurse (CEN) credential, which the Board of Certification for Emergency Nurses (BCEN) administers in the United States and Canada. This organization also publishes a handbook for candidates including its history, eligibility rules, and application process and checklist.

Surgical Technologists

Among other health care professionals who are night owls are the surgical technologists who are members of the team of surgeons, anesthesiologists, registered nurses, and any other medical staff present during surgery. Since people may need surgery at any time, surgical technologists will be involved in shift work and are often on call for emergencies.

In order to become a certified surgical technologist (CST), you will have to successfully complete an accredited program offered at community or junior colleges, vocational schools, universities, in the military, or at certain hospitals. The program lasts from nine to 12 months if you want a diploma or certificate, or two years for an associate degree.

Your course work will include medical terminology, anatomy, physiology, microbiology, and pharmacology. You will also learn about surgical procedures and instruments, fundamentals of surgical care, communication and behavioral sciences, and techniques that are necessary to prepare for surgery.

There are three categories of certified surgical technologists:

1. Scrub Surgical Technologist. These technologists handle all the supplies and instruments during surgery. They

have to be knowledgeable about the surgical procedure and maintain the sterile field.

2. Circulating Surgical Technologist. These specialists obtain any additional equipment or supplies that are required during surgery and provide any necessary assistance to the patient or surgical team.

3. Second Assisting Technologist. These professionals assist the surgeon by providing any technical services, excluding cutting, clamping, or suturing.

In order to become certified, you will have to complete your course work and pass the national surgical technologist certifying exam. This exam is administered by the Liaison Council on Certification for the Surgical Technologist (LCC-ST). You will have to renew your certification every six years by earning education credits or taking the exam again.

The U.S. Bureau of Labor Statistics has predicted a rapid job growth for CSTs to the year 2000 and has ranked the profession as the seventh fastest-growing health-related field in the United States. As a certified surgical technologist, you would be working in hospitals, ambulatory care centers, clinics, surgical centers, and physicians' offices.

Salaries vary according to where you live and how much expertise you possess. The Northeast is the highest-paying area, followed by the South, the Midwest, and the West. In 1990, the average annual salary was $20,800 per year.

Medical Technologists

Medical technologists also fall into the category of night owls, for although they usually work 40 hours a week, these hours may be worked in the evening or at night. Laboratories are often open 24 hours a day, seven days a week, so technologists may have to work weekends and holidays.

These specialists perform laboratory tests, usually under the supervision of a physician, to help detect the cause of disease. Their tests can then lead to a diagnosis and treatment. Technologists conduct routine tests on blood, urine, spinal fluids, and virtually any human substance. They may also test for cholesterol levels, AIDS, or blood glucose. Many of these tests are complicated and may be either chemical or bacteriological in nature. Some technologists may even choose to specialize, for example, in microbiology or blood banks.

Training and Certification

You may qualify as a medical technologist with a bachelor's degree, two years of college, vocational school certification, or armed forces training. If you are still in high school, you should concentrate on biology, math, chemistry, and physics.

When you get to college, take the courses that will be accepted for a medical technologist program that is accredited by the Committee on Allied Health Education and Accreditation (CAHEA) of the American Medical Association (AMA).

Usually this course work includes at least 16 hours in chemistry, biology, computer science, and immunology. Your last year of study will be devoted to clinical training. After you have successfully completed your course work, you will be qualified to take the national certifying exam.

Certification is in one of the following categories:

1. Medical Technologist, MT (ASCP) by the Board of Registry of the American Society of Clinical Pathologists;

2. Medical Technologist, MT (AMT), by the American Medical Technologists;

3. Registered Medical Technologist, RMT, by the International Society for Clinical Laboratory Technology; or

4. Clinical Laboratory Scientists, CLS, by the National Certification Agency for Medical Laboratory Personnel Some states may also require additional licensing or testing.

As a medical technologist, you will be working in the same places as the other health care professionals: in hospitals, HMOs, blood banks, doctors' offices, or independent laboratories. You may also work for private agencies or for the government.

There will be a projected 19 percent job growth for medical technologists by the year 2000. New home laboratory testing procedures and the use of equipment that eliminates the need for humans may influence the job growth rate, but since the general population is aging, there will be a built-in base of need for you in the future.

Earnings

Your salary will depend on your location, experience, and expertise, but recent figures show that entry-level federal government salaries range from about $15,000 to $18,000 a year. The average annual salary is about $23,000.

Since there may be pressure on the job, you will have to be calm, patient, and reliable. You will also have to be accurate, clear thinking, and detail-minded. Sometimes the work can be routine, but you will also be learning new techniques all the time and should realize that your work is extremely important for the diagnosis and treatment of disease.

Emergency Medical Technicians

If you want to be in the health field, but from a different angle, you might want to become an emergency medical technician (EMT). These are the health care professionals who have been called as a result of an accident, heart attack, poisoning, knife or gunshot wound. They rush to the site in an ambulance (or sometimes even in a helicopter), where they administer emergency care before transporting the patient to the hospital.

There are three categories of EMTs with varying areas of responsibilities:

1. EMT-Basic. These specialists will bind wounds, resuscitate, stop bleeding, give oxygen, assist heart attack patients, and even deliver babies.

2. EMT-Intermediate. In addition to the basic skills, these EMTs can control blood pressure with anti-shock trousers or administer shocks to patients whose hearts have stopped.

3. EMT-Paramedic. These professionals can also give drugs to patients and operate more complicated equipment.

Emergency medical technicians are in constant radio contact with medical personnel at the hospital who advise them on more complicated procedures. Once they get the patient to the hospital, EMTs have to report exactly what they did and why.

This job is often stressful because life-and-death decisions have to be made in a hurry and under pressure. People can be seriously injured, poisoned, burned, shot, or in the critical stages of a disease. In addition, EMTs are exposed to life-threatening diseases and must do strenuous lifting, moving, kneeling, and bending. They work irregular hours and are often on call for emergencies.

EMTs work in hospitals, in police and fire departments, or for private companies. In large cities, they are paid for their work; in small towns, they are often volunteers.

In order to become an EMT-Basic, you will need 80 to 120 classroom hours and 10 hours of internship training, usually in a hospital. Instruction will involve heart attacks, bleeding, and fractures. You will also learn how to use basic equipment.

EMT-Intermediates need 35 to 55 hours of additional training, and EMT-Paramedics need between 750 to 2,000 hours of additional training. A high school diploma is a must to qualify for a training program. Also be sure to take driver education and health and sciences courses if you are in high school.

After completing the EMT program, you will have to be certified by your state. You may also want to register as an EMT-Basic with the National Registry of Emergency Medical Technicians or a state agency. After two years, you will have to reregister as a working EMT who has met the necessary continuing education requirements.

Job opportunities look good to the year 2005, especially in hospitals and ambulance services. In 1991, the average annual entry-level salary ranged from about $19,000 to $24,000, depending on location and experience. You may also be interested in the fact that fire departments pay more than other employers.

Profile of an EMT-Paramedic

John Gary has been working as a paramedic for Paramedic Services of Illinois for 1-1/2 years. He'd had an interest in helping other people in some way since he was in high school, but he got sidetracked along the way. For about eight years after high school, he worked as a carpenter and truck driver.

Some friends of his were taking courses at night to become emergency medical technicians-ambulance (EMTAs), and as he was looking through their textbooks, his interest in the work was rekindled. He enrolled in a course to become an EMTA.

John says that in Illinois he had a choice of taking the courses either at a community college or a hospital. The curriculum is identical since it is regulated by the state department of health, but less expensive at the college. In order to enroll in the program, he just had to have a high school diploma; no other prerequisites were required. John does think now, in retrospect, that high school courses in anatomy, biology, and chemistry would have been very helpful to him and would recommend them to anyone considering this line of work. He attended class for six months, two hours a week. And, yes, there was plenty of homework. After he completed his course work, he had to pass a state licensing test to become certified to practice basic life support (BLS) as an EMTA.

He soon realized, however, that EMTAs do not make much money, so he decided to continue his education and become a paramedic who could then administer advanced life support (ALS). In order to become a paramedic, he needed an additional 600 hours of classroom and clinical time. Prerequisites to entering a paramedic training were to first be a very good EMTA, pass the BLS exam, and have six months' experience on an ambulance.

John chose a nine-month course at Loyola, although there are different possibilities for length and intensity of course work, depending on where you study. He attended classes two nights a week for four hours a night.

During that time, on weekends or on nights when he wasn't attending classes, he put in eight hours a week in hospital training. He worked in different hospitals in every department, from the operating room to the emergency room to pediatrics and maternity. During this time, he observed doctors and was allowed to apply his knowledge under supervision.

John said that out of 200 applicants for paramedic school, only 34 were selected, and of that number, only 17 graduated. John thinks that the work is not that difficult, but that you really have to apply yourself and give up a lot of your personal life while you are studying. Also, many people are working full time during the day and going to school at night. Those may be the reasons behind an almost 50 percent dropout rate. He finds, though, that private companies are particularly interested in hiring people with more education and are in many cases prepared to pay for tuition for continuing education.

His course work to become a paramedic included physiology, anatomy, and the study of electrolytes, cells, atoms, trauma, and drug dosage. After he completed his course work, John had to pass a state exam to become a provisional paramedic.

To become a full-fledged paramedic, he could have ridden in an ambulance for 480 hours or completed a specific number of cardiac calls where drugs were administered, a specific number of trauma calls, and so on until the standard number of calls was achieved. There were, in other words, different systems he could choose from.

During this time, he also had to write up reports and meet with his hospital program director once a month to go over the details of his calls. Once he fulfilled these requirements, his hospital program director had to write a letter of recommendation for him to the state licensing board. In addition to all this, he needed a valid driver's license and a good driving record.

John now works for a company that contracts paramedic services to fire departments. He thinks it is easier to move up the career ladder in a private ambulance service because the turnover rate is so high. When you work for a fire department, on the other hand, you can't move up as fast because you are really working within the structure of the fire department, and not within a corporation.

Within five to ten years, John could become a preceptor. Preceptors work with paramedic students and write reports to the program director at the hospital regarding the students' progress. They play a vital role in either recommending or not recommending students for training and certification.

In private companies, John could become a supervisor of EMTAs and paramedics or an instructor of EMTAs or paramedics. If he decided to get into management, he would need at least a B.A. in business administration.

John thinks that a good paramedic has to have a great deal of patience, an ability to deal effectively with a wide variety of people in stressful circumstances, and a good sense of humor. He adds that most medical people, who deal with death on a regular basis, develop a so-called "black" humor to help them cope with the stress. He also believes that you would have to have excellent problem-solving skills because every call is different. Therefore, you have to be flexible and be able to adapt to different emergency situations and patient conditions.

Good paramedics also have to be detail minded because their medical reports must be thorough and accurate. They are considered legal documents and are there for the paramedics' protection.

Since paramedics are often in other people's homes, they also have to be honest. Many times money or other valuables are lying on tables or are otherwise readily available for stealing. John also thinks that paramedics have to be very sincere in dealing with patients and their families. They shouldn't make the mistake of telling anyone that everything will be all right. They can only assure them that the paramedics will do their very best to make them well.

John thinks that paramedics should be physically fit enough to be able to lift and carry patients up and down stairs, haul equipment, or do other heavy work. But he says that the paramedic field is wide open for women, so you don't have to be an Arnold Schwarzenegger to be a paramedic. Sometimes paramedics are resting in the fire house and, literally within seconds, they have to be dressed and ready for action. So there is often a very quick change of pace that requires physical and mental fitness. He now works out regularly, not necessarily just for fitness, but also to release tension.

As you might have guessed, John is a night owl. He works on an every-third-day basis. For example, on Monday, he works from 8 A.M. to 8 A.M.—24 hours in a row. Then he has Tuesday and Wednesday off. On Thursday, he works 24 hours and has

Friday and Saturday off. Then he's back to 24 hours on Sunday, and so on. No matter which days are holidays, birthdays, anniversaries, or graduations, if he's "on," he misses out on those celebrations. But he does say that they eat well at the firehouse on Thanksgiving.

His overnight calls are often police related and generally have something to do with alcohol abuse. Car accidents and assaults seem to be the most common emergencies. In some communities, shootings, stabbings, and gang-related emergencies are common. Sometimes he gets some of his most serious accidents and injuries when he's sound asleep, but once that tone sounds, he's up and running.

John cites the following as advantages to shift work:

- He doesn't have to wait in long lines in stores.

- He can get his car serviced easily and quickly.

- He doesn't have to worry about rush-hour traffic—ever!

- He can make telephone calls anywhere during the day.

- He can make appointments with doctors and dentists almost any time he wants.

Disadvantages to shift work are:

- He has a hard time adjusting his sleeping to the strange hours.

- His wife works regular hours—9 A.M. to 5 P.M. Monday through Friday. This adds some stress to their relationship.

- He misses out on many holidays and special family events.

- He sometimes has to work Friday and Saturday nights when his friends who work regular hours are out partying.

For now, John likes what he is doing—despite the disadvantages. Because the work is so strenuous, however, he is not sure whether he will be able to perform effectively as he gets older. So he does think about furthering his education to be able to eventually get into management. That way, he might even get a good night's sleep.

After looking at all these health-care possibilities, you may now want to begin to assess your aptitudes, qualities, and desires to continue your education and training, in many cases, for quite a few years after high school and even after college. But if you're a night owl with the necessary skills and interests as well as a desire to help others, then health care could be your nighttime niche.

For Further Information

American Medical Association
515 North State St.
Chicago, IL 60610

Association of American Medical Colleges
Publications Department
2450 N St., NW
Washington, DC 20037

American Osteopathic Association
Department of Public Relations
142 East Ontario St.
Chicago, IL 60611

American Academy of Physician Assistants
950 North Washington St.
Alexandria, VA 22314

National Commission of Certification of Physician Assistants, Inc.
2845 Henderson Mill Rd., NE
Atlanta, GA 30341

Division of Allied Health Education and Accreditation
American Academy of Physician Assistants
950 North Washington St.
Alexandria, VA 22314
  Publications include:
    "Information on the Physician Assistant Profession"

American Association of Occupational Health Nurses
(AAOHN)
50 Lenox Pointe
Atlanta, GA 30324
  Publications include:
    The Occupational Health Nurse...Your Key to Managing Health Care Costs
    Ergonomics (AAOHN videotapes)
    "Occupational Health Nursing: The Answer to Health Care Cost
    Containment"
    "Standards of Occupational Health Nursing Practice" (AAOHN
    brochures)

Accreditation Review Committee on Education in Surgical
Technology
7108-C South Alton Way
Englewood, CO 80112

American Association of Blood Banks
1117 North 19th St.
Suite 600
Arlington, VA 2209

American Association of Surgeon's Assistants
1600 Wilson Blvd.
Suite 905
Arlington, VA 22209

American Health Care Association
1201 L St., NW
Washington, DC 20005

American Hospital Association
Division of Nursing
840 North Lake Shore Dr.
Chicago, IL 60611

American Medical Technologists
710 Higgins Rd.
Park Ridge, IL 60068
  Publications include:
    "Medical Technologists" (Brief 16)
    "Blood Bank Specialists" (Brief 71)

American Nurses' Association
2420 Pershing Rd.
Kansas City, MO 64108

American Nurses Publishing (ANP)
600 Maryland Ave., SW
Suite 100 West
Washington, DC 20024
  Publications include:
    *Career Ladders: An Approach to Professional Productivity and Job
    Satisfaction*
    Nursing Education: Enrolling in a College or University
    *Roles and Responsibilities for Nursing Continuing Education
    Across All Settings*
    Standards for Professional Nursing Education
    *Innovation at the Work Site: Delivery of Nurse-Managed Primary Health
    Care Services*

American Society for Medical Technology
2021 L St., NW
Suite 400
Washington, DC 20036

Association of Physician Assistant Programs
950 North Washington St.
Alexandria, VA 22314
   Publications include:
      National Directory of Physician Assistant Programs, 1989-1990
      Physician Assistant Programs Directory, Eleventh Edition, 1992

Association of Surgical Technologists (AST)
7108-C South Alton Way
Englewood, CO 80112
   Publications include:
      "Surgical Technology: A Growing Career" (AST brochure)

Board of Certification for Emergency Nursing
216 Higgins Rd.
Park Ridge, IL 60068

Certification Examination for Emergency Nurses
American College Testing (ACT) (82)
PO Box 168
Iowa City, IA 52243

Chronicle Guidance Publications, Inc.
66 Aurora St.
P.O. Box 1190
Moravia, NY 13118

Emergency Nurses Association (ENA)
216 Higgins Rd.
Park Ridge, IL 60068

National Association for Practical Nurse Education and Service,
Inc. (NAPNES)
1400 Spring St., Suite 310
Silver Spring, MD 20910
> Publications include:
>> *Career Directory for LP/VNs (1989)*
>> "The NAPNES Career Brief"

National Association of Emergency Medical Technicians
9140 Ward Parkway
Kansas City, MO 64114

National League for Nursing
Communications Department
350 Hudson St.
New York, NY 10014

National Student Nurses' Association
555 West 57th St.
Suite 1325
New York, NY 10019

CHAPTER FIVE

The Communications Industry

W hen we say the words "the media," many ideas may come to our minds. We might think of the media as any source of communication, information, or entertainment. We may first think of television because it is right in our home all the time and we probably watch it more than we would like to admit.

But television does provide news and weather reports; dramas and comedies; sporting events; home shopping programs; new and old movies; travel, science, and talk shows; live court action; reruns; educational programs and cartoons. In the not-too-distant future, we are even promised a 500-channel TV set. So television is a major component of the media because it provides us with communication, information, and entertainment. Newspapers, magazines, and radio also meet the definition of media that provide news and entertainment.

All of us are greatly influenced by the various media that fill our days and nights with entertainment and information. We read, listen, and watch for hours every day because these media form the basis of the common knowledge that we receive and react to on a daily basis. In many ways, they form the basis of our society and culture by providing us with the everyday information needed to form opinions, make decisions, and relate to our environment.

Who doesn't turn on a radio every day for the news, weather, traffic reports, or favorite music? Radios are now constant companions, thanks to inexpensive headsets, to joggers, cyclists, commuters, beachcombers, and even people who work at computers all day. Often supervisors allow computer operators to wear headsets to drown out the sound of the machines and to make their work more pleasant.

Who doesn't read a newspaper on the bus or train to work or spend hours on Sunday going through the comics, sports section, book reviews, fashion reports, and, almost incidentally, the hard news coverage and editorials?

And who doesn't spend a few hours after dinner watching sitcoms, news reports, movies, or made-for-TV dramas? Isn't that why the expression "couch potato" was coined?

Kids watch their favorite shows on Saturday morning, and game shows, talk shows, and soaps entertain those who are at home during the day. Cable TV has also opened up new possibilities for community and local shows.

Many of us subscribe to magazines that appeal to one or another topic of interest. Or we can browse through the magazine section of a grocery, drug, or bookstore and find magazines on fashion, health, architecture, nutrition, hobbies, interior design, religion, music, art, news, business, travel, pets, body building, politics, food preparation, parenting, or mechanics.

Magazines may appeal to certain age and interest groups, such as children, women, or senior citizens. They may cater to certain ethnic groups or political affiliations. The range of topics in magazines is as broad and diversified as the range of human experience.

Media Night owls

Who puts all of this together for us to be so informed and entertained? As you might expect, many people of various talents, capabilities, and backgrounds bring all this information and entertainment into our lives. In addition to administrative, supervisory, and clerical personnel, the media need announcers, newscasters, reporters, producers, correspondents, writers, editors, photographers, camera operators, technicians, artists, designers, and printers. And many of these talented individuals are night owls. Let's take a closer look at some of these jobs to determine where you might fit in best.

Reporters

If you have a knack for writing, you may want to become a reporter, editor, columnist, or correspondent. Your hub is the newsroom, which today is a highly automated place to be in. Computers, lasers, and satellites help bring the news to us every day.

The reporter's job is to go to where the news is being made—at the scene of a fire or a crime, at city hall, at a disaster area—and gather the facts by observing and interviewing key people. Who, when, what, where, and why—these are the five "W's" every reporter brings back to the newsroom. If your assignment is to investigate people in government, you may have to thoroughly research public documents, attend public hearings, and interview the people involved.

Reporters may bring tape recorders and notebooks with them, and some may even use portable computers on the scene and send the story by modem to the computer in the newsroom. Often photographers are assigned to accompany the reporter to the story. Television reporters may report a story live or it may be prerecorded. No matter which method is used, reporters are always working on deadline.

As a general assignment reporter, you may work a particular "beat," such as police stations—the crime beat. Other reporters specialize in particular areas of expertise, such as politics, sports, business, real estate, religion, the arts, education, or science. Working as a reporter will bring you into contact with a wide range of people and events. Some will be sad or tragic, such as fires, floods, murders, or disasters. Others will be joyful and uplifting, such as personal triumphs over physical or emotional obstacles, communities working together to rebuild after a natural disaster, or a rescue team that has successfully removed a child from a dangerous situation. The work can make a lifelong career for you or it can be a stepping stone to managerial, political, teaching, or public relations positions.

Reporters who work for a morning newspaper generally will have to work the 4 to 12 shift or the graveyard shift. Radio and TV reporters will work days or evenings. Most reporters are always on call, however, because of deadlines or because news breaks at any time. Reporters on smaller newspapers may have to perform a variety of tasks, including taking photos, writing headlines, or laying out pages. Regardless of the medium, the primary requirements for a reporter are the ability to gather facts, analyze them, and write so that the public can understand the events that take place every day and, as a result, be able to form opinions and make decisions about those events. Reporters play a vital role in our society, especially in guaranteeing one of our most valuable rights—the freedom of the press.

Training and Education

What should you do to become a reporter? The Newspaper Association of America Foundation recommends the following steps:

1. Write, write, write.

2. Study liberal arts.

3. Work as a summer intern.

4. Work on a campus newspaper.

5. Talk to reporters.

Let's take a closer look at each of these recommendations to see if they fit you and your career aptitude.

Practice Writing

What should you write? Anything and everything. Write research papers; write for religious or community groups; write for your school newspapers; write book or movie reviews; write about sporting events; write in your journal or diary.

Study Liberal Arts

You should also try to get the broadest kind of education, with emphasis on language, both English and foreign languages; sociology, economics, political science, history, computers, and journalism. The same type of course work will be helpful in high school. Some journalism courses may include the history of journalism, ethics, basic reporting, and copy editing.

Gain Experience

Both in high school and in college, you will have opportunities to work on your school newspaper. You may not only write for these publications but also learn how to edit or even manage. During the summer vacations, be sure to apply for the internship program on your local newspaper.

Learn from Reporters

While working as an intern, get to know as many reporters, editors, and photographers as possible. Learn as much about their jobs as you can; that is, gather the facts, analyze them, and then decide if the newsroom is the place for you.

Work Pressures

Remember that a reporter is under constant pressure to meet deadlines. The Newspaper Guild adds the pressure of shift work as one of the disadvantages of the reporter's job. Although there may be a pay differential for night work, the guild feels that the adjustments of the social and biological rhythms associated with shift work do not compensate for the additional pay. One of its locals even found in a survey that night workers suffer more health and sleep-related problems than day workers. But, as with any other career that you love, most reporters would probably not give up their job for a little more sleep.

Earnings

The Newspaper Guild also reports the following salaries for reporters: starting pay for reporters and photographers on most daily newspapers range from $300 to $650 a week. For more experienced professionals, the range is from $450 to more than $1,000 a week. Depending on the size of the radio station, reporters' salaries range from about $12,000 to $36,000, with the average annual salary about $15,000. These are general figures and will vary wherever you work.

Profile of a Television News Writer/Producer

One of the first things you would notice about Tim Jackson, writer/producer for WGN-TV, Chicago, is his great voice. Right away, you think that he must be an actor, announcer, or news anchor; his voice fills the room with a beautiful sound. But when he was younger, Tim says, he was just considered loud! Well, Tim took that voice (and various other skills) and made an exciting career for himself in radio and television.

As a teenager, Tim had his first night-owl job, but he hated the hours. He vowed never to work overnight again. Then, when he was just 17, he was doing voice-overs for commercials even though he'd had no formal speech courses. His uncle had encouraged him, though, which eventually led him to doing literally thousands of hours of voice-overs for the Northern Trust Bank's industrial training program, consisting of cassettes and slide shows.

Tim attended college in New Jersey, where he studied liberal arts, public speaking, and theater. After taking a year off, he continued his education at Columbia College in Chicago, where he studied broadcasting and writing. While there, Tim worked as an intern for a local radio station. He was a general, all-round "gopher," but he also learned to write and edit promotional copy and assist the producer.

But Tim's first real dream was to be a radio disc jockey. Tim loved music and thought it would be his niche. After many rejections, however, this rather sensitive person decided this was not for him. He took a job as an overnight assignment editor at the radio station, where he continued to learn new skills and gain valuable experience.

He later accepted the news bureau chief position for a new satellite news project—a joint venture of Westinghouse and ABC-TV. It was going to be competition for the emerging CNN headline news shows. Tim had a five-state territory to build in a somewhat hostile environment.

Because the new venture wanted its affiliates to provide the product free of charge, Tim met with a great many problems. He was working impossibly long hours, seven days a week, and his work was mostly administrative. Administrative work was not what he really wanted to do because he had other talents he wanted to utilize, not the least of which was that voice. And by this time, he knew he wanted to be a news writer and producer.

He had produced and written four or five different late night radio shows, co-written live entertainment shows, and produced radio specials. So after 11-1/2 months with the satellite news project, which folded after about 14 months, Tim was looking for a job.

He had applied for a job at WGN-TV more than once, but this time he got lucky. They offered him a job as a news writer working from 4 A.M. to noon. So even though as a teenager Tim vowed never again to work the night shift, the career that he loves brings him back to nights all the time. From his many years in both radio and television, he has become accustomed to every imaginable shift, including 6 A.M. to 1 P.M. and 1 A.M. to 9 A.M., wherever there is a demand.

What does Tim now find so appealing about working at night? First, he is an independent, creative, and imaginative person—all qualities needed for the overnight shift. Since there may not be as many people on the overnight staff, he often has to wear many hats. For instance, he has to know how to write interesting copy, how to match up the words with the graphics, and how to put together the best possible product under the pressure of tight deadlines.

Producers also have to keep up with the latest and ever-changing technological advances in computers, cameras, and telephone systems. For example, WGN was one of the first TV news studios to use the computer. When Tim was hired, he was not computer literate and had to learn very quickly. He advises anyone who is coming into this business to learn as many computer systems as possible and to become familiar with both IBM and Macintosh, notebook and desktop platforms and be willing to learn new programs as they become available.

Advantages and Disadvantages

Tim believes that he has received more opportunities by being willing to work the graveyard shift because there is less competition for these jobs—therefore more possibilities to be resourceful. But if you are looking at overnight work because of the pay differential, you are going into it for the wrong reason. It simply isn't that big.

One advantage, though, is that there is generally no top-level management working the overnight shift, so you can be independent, self-reliant, and creative in your work. Tim also likes not having to fight rush-hour traffic and being able to make appointments during the day with comparative ease.

You will not be surprised, however, if Tim lists sleep deprivation as one of the major disadvantages of overnight work. He also cites isolation, lack of patience, and burnout of the senses as some of the problems with night work. He advises night owls to take frequent naps and breaks and to watch out for weight gain.

Tim also suggests that anyone interested in radio or television news writing, reporting, or producing should get a good, solid education. Today's employers are looking for people with at least a bachelor's degree, and a master's degree is even better. What does he recommend studying as an undergraduate? He suggests communications, writing, history, political science, law, and literature. And because Tim sees the global implications in news reporting, studying foreign languages, living in foreign countries, and knowing world geography is also becoming more and more necessary. He also emphasizes reading, preferably the classics, and writing, writing, writing if you want to be successful in this field.

Future Trends

What do you have to look forward to in the near future as far as working conditions are concerned? Tim believes that you will have to be computer literate and be willing to work flexible hours. He sees a trend toward hiring more part time employees because more and more employers are unwilling to pay benefits. And although more opportunities will arise, there will probably be more work for less pay.

He also says that you should know that this business is market driven; that is, it supplies the product for the demand. For instance, if you want to be a network news anchor, you have to be aware that your "look" is sometimes as important as, or in some markets more important than, reportorial skills. And the "look" can change overnight.

The need for night owls may also dry up if the demand dries up. Overnight shifts are important as long as people want to hear the news, weather, or music on the morning drive. If the public no longer wants or needs that, you'll be working the day shift. But if you love this work, as Tim obviously does, the hours won't matter. As long as you have the energy to put out a new product every day that is as creative as you can make it, you'll do well in this field.

Editors

But perhaps you'd like to think about becoming an editor. First we'll take a look at what an editor is and then we'll look at the different kinds of editors. Editors for any of the media must have an excellent command of the English language, a keen mind for detail, and a sharp eye for error in fact or discrepancy in logic. Editors also may have to deal with budgetary needs and have an ability to motivate others on the staff to do their best job.

City editors assign stories to reporters and decide which stories should be emphasized. City editors are key players in the newsroom who have to make decisions quickly and who need a challenge in their work.

Copy editors check written articles, or "copy," for errors in grammar, writing style, and fairness in presentation. They may also be required to know something about photo editing and layout.

Feature editors assist in the development of stories that affect the readers' emotions in some way. These specialists are interested in human behavior and motivation, as well as lifestyles. Newspapers may also have specialty editors for food, sports, movies, the arts, and education.

Editorial page editors record the newspaper's philosophy, opinion, and beliefs. Sometimes they endorse political candidates; sometimes they draw attention to injustice, corruption, or graft in government, the courts, corporations, or even the educational system.

Managing editors oversee the daily operation of newsrooms and generally work daytime hours unless a major story is breaking. These professionals know not only what good copy and writing style are all about, they also have to know about all the functions of the newsroom, understand how to motivate people, and want to make a difference in the community.

Training and Education
Many editors started out as editorial assistants, research assistants, or trainees. Writers and editors need highly developed research skills, and it's a good idea to have a wide range of knowledge and interests. They may also be required to understand layout, graphics, and interviewing techniques. Computer skills are a must now in the newsroom.

You should have a college degree to become a writer, editor, or reporter. Most employers prefer a degree in English, journalism, or communications. If you decide to specialize in business, religion, or politics, you should also take courses in those subjects.

Graphic Artists and Page Designers

If news breaks in the middle of the night, a newsroom needs more than reporters and editors to get the story out on time. News photographers and artists are also needed to bring the facts of the story to life. Artists may have to graphically represent an earthquake, fire, courtroom scene, or police emergency. They may use desktop computers to design maps, charts, tables, and even cartoons.

Computer graphics are now much needed in newsrooms for informational graphics. These graphics might depict how something was done as well as where it happened. They also may represent a certain perspective or collection of events to be analyzed. A good news artist has the ability to visually depict or back up a story with computer-generated graphics coupled with the ability to work with reporters and editors to help tell the story or represent the facts.

Page designers are needed for newspapers to clearly and artistically present the whole story—text and graphics. In order to do that, the page designer must understand typography and the skillful use of photos, maps, and diagrams. Page designers have to know about the news as well as about art.

News Photographers

Most of us in the 20th century have become accustomed to some sort of graphic representation either to supplant the printed word or to complement it. Photographers have done a great deal in the past century to help us see and interpret the newspaper's words in a different light and perspective. In fact, we have become accustomed to the "picture that is worth 1,000 words."

News photographers have to be where the news breaks—whenever that happens. It could be in their own hometown or halfway around the world. It could be a war or a major sporting event. It could be the fall of the Berlin Wall or an economic summit in Italy. News can happen at any time and any place, and a photographer will be there to record it.

Photographers, who take still photographs, and camera operators, who operate video and movie cameras, not only have to develop a feel for the story, they also have to be technically proficient with cameras and their various paraphernalia. Photographers generally use 35-millimeter cameras. Camera operators use 16-millimeter cameras or camcorders. Both may need filters, flashes, zoom lenses, and tripods to create special effects.

Training and Education

You would do well to take some photography classes at either community, junior, or four-year colleges to become a photographer or camera operator. Working in a camera shop during summer vacations, taking photos at family gatherings, or working on your high school yearbook will give you some experience with photography, film, and photo techniques. You will then receive on the-job training at newspapers or TV and radio stations.

As with most other professions, however, the more formal education you receive, the more opportunities you will have to get a better job with more possibilities for advancement. That education, along with practical experience, will put you in a good career position.

Be sure to hone your computer skills, including familiarity with graphics software. Learn about production, design, and technical rendering. Keep your eyes open for photo opportunities and take pictures of everything. Or draw them. Just as writers must write, photographers and graphic artists must expand their visual possibilities in order to succeed. You'll have to be able to tell a story with your picture, capture the dramatic moment, and communicate a feeling for the event. This will take practice, but you will have many career opportunities with the media if you develop these skills.

Earnings

Salaries will vary from location to location and with the size of the newsroom. Larger cities and facilities will generally pay more than suburban or rural locations, but they will give you valuable experience and a foot in the door of your profession.

Radio, Television, and New Technology

Newspapers need all these professionals, but TV and radio stations need them and more. Both need announcers or anchors and broadcast technicians. Cable TV is opening more and more opportunities for careers, and interactive technology will offer new challenges in the future for the crossover of media and entertainment. Some newspapers and magazines are already interactive, thanks to the networking system that links so-called global villages and creates the concept of multimedia. This networking on the information superhighway is creating new job possibilities now and will continue to do so in the future.

But first let's take a look at some of the career possibilities that are available now to night owls. Probably the most visible or audible people to those of us watching or listening are the announcers. These people may be called anchors, disc jockeys, talk show hosts, sportscasters, weather forecasters, or commentators. They are all vital links between us and the outside world. We often pick our favorites and listen to or watch them on a regular basis. Their style, appearance, voice, attitude, and even sense of humor bring us back to them. They eventually form a major part of our daily lives, and if they leave the station or network and go somewhere else, we will invariably find them. They can and do have very loyal fans.

Disc jockeys often become so popular that they could be called cult figures. They're the ones who play the music we like the best, read the commercials, sometimes give us the news and weather, often host guest interviews, and always inject their personalities, comments, and opinions into their time slot. That's when we really get to know them and begin to build our loyalty to them. They are usually glib and can fill in the time with amusing and informative banter about a wide range of current events and popular opinions.

News anchors are usually reporters who read the news stories and present any prerecorded material to the listening or viewing audience. Often they present their stories live at the scene of the news event. This often happens with natural disasters, fires, or accidents.

The people who predict the weather are also called meteorologists. Their information is usually received from national satellite transmissions or from local weather sources.

Sportscasters can report live from the locker room, stadium, golf course, or tennis court. They may cover the Olympics or the World Cup at sites throughout the world. Or they may be assigned to the local Little League game or the high school volleyball championship. They often conduct postgame interviews with key players or coaches and offer commentaries on strategy and game plan. Their work may be presented live or on tape.

Radio stations and television networks also offer viewpoints and opinions about events that take place locally, nationally, or internationally. Since news anchors are supposed to present the news—that is, without injecting their personal opinions on the news—these opinions are expressed by news analysts or commentators. Anchors and reporters may serve as commentators, but they must tell the listeners or viewers when they are acting as commentators. Many news shows will have a specific segment that is devoted to nothing but opinion, but that is clearly stated at the outset of that segment.

The Work Experience

Radio stations and television networks are generally on 24 hours a day, so media people should expect some shift work. Many disc jockeys and talk show hosts work through the night; some handle the very early morning shift. The same problems of sleep deprivation and loss of some social life can, therefore, bring stress into the workplace.

Again, if you are doing what you love, you will find other rewards. One may be that fan loyalty. Another may be the recognition and esteem that you earn in the community. Still another may be your ability to influence people's lives and enhance them through your insights, personality, or trustworthiness.

Training and Education

How do you get to be an announcer? There are a few paths open to you if you choose radio or television announcing. Let's start with courses you should seriously consider taking while you are in high school. You should definitely master English—grammar, pronunciation, and writing. Speech and drama classes, public speaking, and even foreign languages also will be valuable.

If you think you may want to be a sportscaster, start now to learn about different sports and sports figures. If you want to be a disc jockey, start learning about music, including instruments and famous musicians. Learn to differentiate the various kinds of music, such as country, rap, rock, folk, big band, jazz, and rhythm and blues. Or, if you prefer classical music, know the difference between an opera and an operetta, Domingo and Carreras, Mozart and Wagner, a symphony and a concerto.

If you want to be a news anchor, read the newspapers and news magazines regularly and become familiar with current events. If there are any apprenticeship programs at your local radio stations or TV networks, apply to work with them during summer vacations.

Cable TV has expanded the opportunities for public access shows, which are locally produced. These may have work experience programs for students during weekends or summers. They may even offer financial assistance for further study or on-the-job training. In other words, your time outside the classroom and in extracurricular activities can be used as learning time, too.

After high school, you may want to enroll in a four-year college or broadcasting school. A bachelor's degree in journalism, broadcast journalism, communications, or telecommunications would be advisable. Be sure to check the credentials of any technical school before you enroll, and consider also community colleges for the courses you may need.

What It Takes

As important as all your degrees, diplomas, and certificates, however, are some personal qualities, such as personality, voice, and, for TV, appearance. To demonstrate these qualities, you will probably be asked to submit an audition tape, either video or audio, to be considered as an announcer. But don't be surprised if you have to work your way up to being an announcer, beginning perhaps as a production assistant, reporter, research assistant, or interviewer.

Timing is everything in the broadcast studio, and you will have to be able to present your story in specific sound bites. You may also have to work under the pressure of deadlines. Your facility with English has to be excellent, and your knowledge of the local, national, and international scene has to be constantly updated, especially in your specific field—music, weather, sports, or news.

Career Paths

Because of the rapid revolution and advances in technology, new networks and cable systems will probably provide more work for radio and television announcers. As an entry-level broadcaster, you may want to start out in radio and then branch out to other media, keeping in mind that overall, communications is a highly competitive field. You may want to get some solid experience in the smaller markets, prove yourself as a capable announcer, and then try for the larger radio stations and television studios.

Earnings

Network announcers can command fairly high wages, so the competition may be fierce for the top jobs. You may have to be patient and work for smaller stations at first where you can develop your skills, style, and basic abilities before you are on the air.

It is difficult to talk about salaries because they differ considerably, depending on whether you are working in radio, network, or cable TV. Salaries vary as much by where your work—whether in a small town or a large city—as by your training and experience. You may start out with not too much money in your paycheck, but the possibilities of becoming a player in the national networks is always there if you are willing to work hard for it.

Behind the Scenes:
Technicians and Engineers

Behind the scenes at the station or studio are less visible people, but they are no less important than the anchor. These are the broadcast technicians, without whom we would never get the news, sports, weather, or music. These highly skilled professionals are responsible for installing and operating the equipment that makes the programs possible. This equipment includes cameras, microphones, lighting, sound effects, tape recorders, and film editors. This is all done in the control room of the station or studio.

From the control room, the technicians move from camera to camera, from taped to live presentations, signaling directions to others with their hands or through headsets. Their main responsibilities are to be sure that the mechanics of production are in place so that the programs can be transmitted.

There are various types of technicians (also called operators or engineers), each with specific functions. For example, there are audio and video control engineers as well as recording engineers. These technicians control the quality of sound and picture and make sure the correct sound effects are produced through the operation of specialized equipment. Other technicians keep the equipment in good condition through repair and servicing.

Chief engineers generally supervise the engineering and other technical personnel, but in cable television they have additional responsibilities. For cable, they are in charge of all technical work involved in cable system design, equipment, layout for communications service, standards for all equipment and materials, and construction of facilities.

They also may make suggestions for new products, assist in marketing, advise on matters of franchise renewal, and help in budget preparation. You would need a degree in electrical engineering or comparable experience to qualify for this position.

The chief technician supervises all the technicians and is responsible for assuring the highest quality signal delivery of satellite and microwave relays to the head-end. The head-end holds the antennae that broadcast these signals. As supervisors, these technicians set quality standards for the staff's performance and handle all personnel problems, including handling salary reviews. Requirements for this position include a background in the industry and electronic training, plus experience in the field.

Training and Education

If you want to become a technician, it is a good idea to get formal training at a technical school, community college, or four-year college. Your degree should be in broadcast technology, although for some jobs, a degree in electronics or engineering would apply. In high school, it would be a good idea to take classes in math and electronics, develop hobbies that allow you to learn about electronics and electronic equipment, and develop good eye-hand coordination.

If you operate transmitters, you will have to get a permit from the Federal Communications Commission (FCC). You will also receive further on-the-job training from more experienced technicians once you are hired. And you will almost certainly start out at smaller stations where you will gain valuable experience and training so that you can advance to the larger studios. You may eventually want to be certified by the Society of Broadcasting Engineers once you gain some experience—and passed their exam, of course. Salaries vary according to location (with the larger markets paying the highest salaries), experience, position, and training.

Producers, Directors, and Managers

According to the National Cable Television Association, cable TV also needs producers, assistant directors, and floor managers. Producers may be called on to select the cast, schedule rehearsals, write the script, and direct the camera staff regarding shots, angles, and cameras.

Assistant directors' responsibilities include putting the proper equipment in place before production, timing the show, and working with the director and crew during the show. This position requires a bachelor's degree in communications and some previous experience in production. The floor manager acts as liaison between the control room and the cast.

Cable TV can be found in about 60 percent of households with television sets, and it is proving to be formidable competition to the major networks. It is a "boom" that is surely here to stay. Part of the reason is the diversity of programming available, including community shows, 24-hour news programs, college courses, old and new films, home shopping programs, sporting events, and nature shows.

Cable TV now employs more than 91,000 full-time employees. This number will grow because of new systems being built and the increasing sophistication of cable programming. Cable TV programs, such as major sporting events, can also be telecast simultaneously throughout the world.

Training and Education

According to the National Cable Television Association, the cable industry is trying to fulfill the growing need for skilled professionals in the field by giving more on-the-job training and providing more training schools. The industry is also looking for engineers with either a bachelor's or master's degree.

Nontechnical positions require a bachelor's degree in business administration, with emphasis in marketing, advertising, or finance, as appropriate to the position. A bachelor's degree in communications or telecommunications, specializing in journalism, radio and television, or communications media would be appropriate for editorial and other nontechnical positions.

Special Educational Opportunities in Communications Media

If you are a member of a minority, have a college degree, and have worked in an unrelated field for at least three years, you may be eligible for fellowships in the cable TV industry. If you are interested, send your resume to the Walter Kaitz Foundation, 660 13th St., Suite 200, Oakland, CA 93612.

The National Cable Television Institute conducts continuing education programs for technological skills. These are available to people who are already employed in the industry. They offer a combination of correspondence courses, self-study courses, and seminars. Some cable companies may provide tuition reimbursement for current employees wanting to take these courses, but those just entering the industry also may be eligible. If you are interested, contact the National Cable Television Institute, Box 27277, Denver, CO 80227-0277, 303/761-8554.

Advanced cable courses are available through Women in Cable, in conjunction with the University of Denver's Center for Management Development. For information, contact Women in Cable, 500 North Michigan Ave., Suite 1400, Chicago, IL 60611.

How to Find a Job

Some recommendations for finding jobs in the radio and television industry are the following:

1. Look in your telephone book for cable systems in your area. If you can't find a listing, check *TV Factbook,* which is published by *Television Digest.* This book lists all cable systems in the United States and Canada and can be found in your library. It comes in two volumes.

2. Get information about cable service in your area from your city government.

3. Go to your local library and look for industry publications that may list job openings.

4. Talk with people who already work in the industry, especially those who have the kind of jobs you're looking for.

5. Talk with representatives at job fairs at school or at work.

6. Find out from local stations if they have internships programs for students during summer vacations.

Somewhere, in all these systems, there are plenty of jobs for night owls. Be sure you find the job you want, and the hours will follow.

For Further Information

Asian American Journalists Association
1765 Sutter St.
Room 1000
San Francisco, CA 94115

American Newspaper Publishers Association Foundation
The Newspaper Center
Box 17407
Dulles National Airport
Washington, DC 20041

American Society of Magazine Editors
575 Lexington Ave.
New York, NY 10022

American Society of Magazine Photographers
419 Park Ave. South
New York, NY 10016

Associated Photographers International
5855 Green Valley Circle
Suite 109
Culver City, CA 90230

Broadcast Education Association
1771 N St., NW
Washington, DC 20036

Cabletelevision Advertising Bureau (CAB)
757 3rd Ave.
New York, NY 10017

Cable Television Administration and Marketing Society
(CTAM)
635 Slaters Lane
Alexandria, VA 22209

Cable Alliance for Education (Cable in the Classroom)
1900 Beauregard St.
Suite 108
Alexandria, VA 22311

Cable Television Public Affairs Association (CTPAA)
1525 Wilson Blvd.
Suite 550
Rosslyn, VA 22209

The Dow Jones Newspaper Fund, Inc.
P.O. Box 300
Princeton, NJ 08543-0300

Eastman Kodak
Kodak Information Center
Department 841
343 State St.
Rochester, NY 14650

Federal Communications Commission
1919 M St., NW
Washington, DC 20554

National Association for Minorities in Cable (NAMIC)
Number 2 Embarcadero Center
Suite 840
San Francisco, CA 94111

National Association of Broadcasters Employment Clearinghouse
1771 N St., NW
Washington, DC 20036

National Association of Hispanic Journalists
National Press Building
Suite 1193
529 14th St., NW
Washington, DC 20045

National Black Media Coalition Resource Center
38 New York Ave., NE
Washington, DC 20002

National Cable Television Association
1724 Massachusetts Ave., NW
Washington, DC 20036

National Federation of Local Cable Programmers (NFLCP)
P.O. Box 27290
Washington, DC 20038-7290

Native American Journalists Association
230 10th Ave. South
Suite 301
Minneapolis, MN 55415

The Newspaper Guild
8611 Second Ave.
Silver Spring, MD 20910

Professional Photographers of America, Inc.
1090 Executive Way
Des Plaines, IL 60018

Radio-Television News Directors Association
1717 K St., NW
Suite 615
Washington, DC 20006

Society of Broadcast Engineers
7002 Graham St.
Suite 216
Indianapolis, IN 46220

Society for Technical Communications, Inc.
901 North Stuart St.
Suite 304
Arlington, VA 22203

Women in Cable
500 North Michigan Ave.
Suite 1400
Chicago, IL 60611

Walter Kaitz Foundation
660 13th St.
Suite 200
Oakland, CA 94612

Periodicals

Advertising Age. 220 East 42nd St., New York, NY 10017.
Broadcast Engineering. P.O. Box 12901, Overland Park, KS 66212.
Broadcasting Magazine. 1705 DeSales St., NW, Washington, DC 20036.
Cablevision Magazine. 825 7th Ave., New York, NY 10019.
Cable World. 1905 Sherman St., Denver, Co 80203.
Career Opportunities News. Garrett Park Press, Garrett Park, MD 20896.
Careers, Focusing on Tomorrow. (newsletter). College Media Review
    Headquarters, Journalism Department, Memphis State University,
    Memphis, TN 38152.
Communications Daily. 2115 Ward Court, NW, Washington, DC 20037.
Communications Week. 1222 National Press Building, Washington, DC
    20045.
Electronic Media. 740 North Rush St., Chicago, IL 60611.
Hollywood Reporter. 6715 Sunset Blvd., Hollywood, CA 90028.
INFOWORLD. InfoWorld Publishing Company, 155 Bovet Rd., Suite
    800, San Mateo, CA 94402.
Multichannel News. 7 East 12th St., New York, NY 10003.

Satellite Business News. 1050 17th St., NW, Washington, DC 20036.
Transmedia Partners. 50 South Steele St., Denver, CO 80209.
Variety. 475 Park Ave. South, New York, NY 10016.

Books and Other Publications

Career Associates. *Career Choices for the 90s: For Students of Communications and Journalism.* New York: Walker and Co., 1990.

Directory of Special Programs for Minority Group Members: Career Information Services, Employment Skills Banks, Financial Aid Sources. Garrett Park Press, P.O. Box 190F, Garrett Park, MD, 1990.

Eddings, Joshua. *How the Internet Works.* California: Ziff-Davis Press, 1994.

Facts About Newspapers. Newspaper Association of America, Fulfillment Department, The Newspaper Center, 11600 Sunrise Valley Dr., Reston, VA 22091.

Financial Aid for Minority Students in Journalism and Mass Communications. Garrett Park Press, P.O. Box 190, Garrett Park, MD 20896.

Internship Directory. Southern Newspaper Publishers Association, Information Department, P.O. Box 28875, Atlanta, GA 30328, 1991.

Journalism and Mass Communication College Search Service. The Dow Jones Newspaper Fund, P.O. Box 300, Princeton, NJ 08543.

Journalism Career and Scholarship Guide. The Dow Jones Newspaper Fund, P.O. Box 300, Princeton, NJ 08543.

Journalism Career Guide for Minorities. The Dow Jones Newspaper Fund, P.O. Box 300, Princeton, N.J. 08543.

National Directory of High School Journalism Workshops for Minority Students. The Dow Jones Newspaper Fund, P.O. Box 300, Princeton, NJ 08543.

The Next Step, Toward Diversity in the Newspaper Business. Newspaper Association of America Foundation and The Poynter Institute of Media Studies, The Newspaper Center, 11600 Sunrise Valley Dr., Reston, VA 22091.

Preparing for a Career in Newspapers. The American Society of Newspaper Editors Foundation, P.O. Box 17004, Washington, DC 20041.

CHAPTER SIX

The Entertainment Industry

L ife would be dreary if all we had to do was work, even when we love our work. The daily routine of waking up to that dreaded alarm clock, drinking our coffee, taking a shower, figuring out what we'll wear, getting on the train or bus, sitting at our desk all day, going home, fixing dinner—or breakfast, if you're a night owl—getting ready for the next day, and going to bed can be tedious on a regular basis.

And even though night owls don't always have "normal" weekends off, they do look forward to their days off to relax, catch up on sleep, go to a show, attend a concert, or rent a movie. Whether the "weekend" comes on Saturday and Sunday or Monday and Wednesday, most working people do think about the "weekend" during their work week as a time to refresh their bodies and rejuvenate their minds.

For some, it even becomes a matter of "living for the weekend." And before it arrives, they have planned for it by discussing it with friends and family, buying tickets to the theater or concert, and making dinner reservations. Or they rush to the video rental store right after work to be sure to get their favorite movie. Or they hurry home to watch their favorite TV show.

Some people will even subscribe to a series of opera or ballet tickets just to be sure that their leisure time entertains them in their preferred form. And the movie houses are packed as soon as a new movie comes out.

On those precious weekends, we can escape into another world of excitement, glamour, adventure, thrills, beauty, and special effects. All of these things come to us via the wonderful world of entertainment, including movies, plays, television shows, concerts, opera, ballet, night club performances, music festivals, and musical comedies.

The variety of available choices only makes it more difficult to decide what to do in our free time. But somehow, even with all these choices, we are able to find something to amuse or entertain us.

That's when we are grateful to the actors, dancers, and musicians, theater managers, projectionists, producers, directors, stagehands, ushers, concession attendants, and box office attendants. They allow us to forget for a short while all the problems, stresses, and worries of the work week. They take us outside of our small world and help us to enjoy the pleasures of artistic talent and professional achievement. And they make it possible for us to return to the routine of the work week more relaxed and invigorated.

Since most plays, operas, concerts, and dance performances are at night, we have many night owls to thank for making our lives more pleasant. Movie houses are open at night, as well as night clubs and music halls. Actors, dancers, and musicians all rehearse during the day, but the show goes on at night, and often into the wee small hours of the morning when the rest of the world is just getting up.

Night Owl Entertainers

Now if you have an inkling, a talent, or an itch to get into show business, there are a lot of possibilities open to you. For some jobs, you will need artistic talent as well as training or education. For others, you might have to acquire supervisory, technical, or organizational skills. But if you want to be in show business, you will soon realize that there's no business like it in the world. So let's get started looking at the possibilities and opportunities available to you as a night owl.

Actors

Probably everybody at one time or another has had the fantasy of being a star, either in the movies, on Broadway, or on a favorite television show. Maybe just for a day it would be fun to see ourselves on the big or small screen or imagine ourselves before a live audience applauding our performance and shouting for more.

Or perhaps we see ourselves in a huge house in Hollywood with a garage full of expensive cars and closets full of fabulous clothes. Everywhere we go, our fans would follow, begging for our autograph. Photographers would hound us for an exclusive picture for their magazine or newspaper. We would be on all the television talk shows, and everyone would love us.

Is this a realistic picture of the working actor, or do only a few talented people fit into that picture? And would you be one of them? Let's take a look at what training it takes to get on stage to become that star.

What It Takes

You have to have some talent that can be developed in order to succeed in the competitive world of show business. You need to be able to interpret your character, memorize your lines and stage directions, and take instructions from your director. You will have to be able to bring your own life experiences or ability to understand human emotions and reactions to your role.

Your facial expressions, gestures, and movements will help you to convey feelings to the audience.

For some roles, you may have to display your singing voice or your dancing feet. Still others may require great physical agility and fitness. Some plays will take place in a modern setting; others may be set in some other century, country, or entire civilization. Some may take place in outer space or in a totally imaginary location.

You may have to research some major historical event or person in order to understand your role. You may have to juggle, fence, swing from the rafters, or play the saxophone.

Your role may require wearing costumes that you could never imagine yourself in. Or you may have to work with strange or awkward props or talk to someone who isn't there. You may be called on to portray a physically or mentally impaired person.

You may have to memorize hundreds of lines or just be a walk-on with no lines. You may play the leading role or a supporting character. More likely, you may start out as an extra, as part of the crowd in movies or plays. Extras are hired through a casting agency, which supplies movie studios with just the number and types they need for that particular movie.

What to Expect

Stardom doesn't come easily, and those fancy cars don't appear overnight in your garage. Many actors, even very talented ones, have to support themselves with some other job or jobs while they establish their reputations. Still others may wait for years before they get steady work.

Since you may have to wait long periods of time between acting jobs, you need to develop patience. Your jobs will depend on auditions, so you must be able to present your talent under pressure and in a comparatively short period of time. The threat of rejection is always hanging over the head of the actor.

Therefore, you will also have to both develop thick skin and maintain your faith in your talent and training. Overnight sensations are rare in this field. Usually actors have to labor in bit parts and infrequent jobs before they begin to get reliable employment.

In the chapter on communications, we discussed the fact that news anchors have to have a "look," and that "look" may be fleeting. This may happen with acting, too. Appearance is very important on the stage and in movies, especially if you want to be a leading man or woman. However, the range of character or supporting roles is much broader and allows for many different shapes, sizes, and ages. So even if you aren't picture perfect, you still can have a long and rewarding career as an actor.

You will also need flexibility in this business because each role can be entirely different from the last one. You have to be mentally prepared to "become" another person. That's called stretching, and you'll have to be able to stretch your talent into a variety of roles. If you are working another job to support yourself, you may need to arrange for flexible hours, too, in case you have to rehearse at odd hours.

You may not only have to work at night, but you also may be part of a traveling company, which requires a great deal of stamina and an ability to adapt to different circumstances. Most movies are now usually shot on location rather than on the back lot of a Hollywood studio. Shooting movies also demands working unusual hours under sometimes adverse conditions in all different climates. So be sure you really love to act before you think about becoming a star.

How to Find Work

Most actors work through a manager or agent who helps guide their careers and find jobs for them—for a fee, of course. Professional actors will probably be members of Actors' Equity

Association, a labor union for stage actors. But even Equity admits that 85 percent of its members are unemployed at any given time—85 percent! So much for those fabulous clothes.

This organization has three ways to become a member: through signing an Equity contract, through their membership candidate program, or through their open door admissions policy. Since so many of the members may be temporarily unemployed at any time, the dues are kept comparatively low.

Other unions that help negotiate contracts and set salaries and working conditions are the Screen Actors Guild (SAG), the Screen Extras Guild (SEG), and the American Federation of Television and Radio Artists (AFTRA). Members of SAG and SEG work in the movies, films, television, and commercials; AFTRA members, in radio and television.

Training and Education

Now that you have seen that there is no guarantee for success or stardom simply by becoming an actor, and you still want to become one, let's take a look at some possible avenues to that stage door or movie camera. Maybe you will join the lucky 15 percent whom we refer to as working actors.

Starting in high school, or earlier, get involved in school plays. See if you really like to memorize lines, follow stage directions, display emotions in public, and accept audience reaction to your performance, whether good or bad. It will get you ready for the real critics down the road.

Work with your drama club, take speech and English classes, and especially literature courses. It is important to begin observing people and how they react to life's situations. Now is the time to become aware of what motivates people to act and react as they do. You could also study different types of people, just in case you have to portray such a person on stage.

This is also a time for you to read all kinds of plays and attend live performances, if possible. You do not have to confine yourself to British and American plays. Many excellent plays have been translated into English from foreign languages all over the world, allowing you to see life and people from different perspectives. Put yourself into different characters' shoes to determine what makes them tick.

Then, by the time you get to college, you will want to major in theater arts. Your course work will probably include a basic liberal arts curriculum with emphasis on the playwright's craft, production, design, and history of the theater, as well as drama and acting classes. Some people also take dancing and singing classes, especially if they want to perform in musicals.

You will also have to audition for roles. If you didn't get the role you wanted, work backstage. If there is a local community theater, audition there, too. In the summer, you might find a job in a summer stock company in resort towns or in some suburbs. There are also possibilities to hone your skills in dinner theaters in cities, suburbs, and rural areas.

You may choose to go to a school that specializes in training actors solely in the craft of acting. These are called dramatic arts schools and are located in most major cities. The best ones are probably located in New York and Los Angeles because these are the creative hubs of the United States.

Most major employers of actors are also located in New York and Los Angeles, and because of that, these are the most competitive cities for acting jobs in this country. But since you do not need a college degree to be an actor, these schools might be the best choice for you. Just be sure to enroll in one with a good reputation.

Earnings

Chances are, you won't make a fortune as an actor, no matter how late you work or how talented you are. But if you do make it to Broadway, recent salary figures for minimum salary was $850 a week. If you make it to "off-Broadway," the salary goes down. However, if you work in the traveling company, you will be paid about $80 more a day. Since your normal work week on the stage consists of eight performances a week, you would also be paid for any additional performances.

Movie and television actors recently received a daily rate of $448, with additional pay for reruns. Pay is usually low on an annual basis because there are so many periods of unemployment in an actor's life. So just because some big Hollywood stars can command millions of dollars per picture, that is not what most actors earn in a lifetime.

Even though you have always wanted to be a star, you will have to realize that stardom doesn't come easily, and sometimes it doesn't come at all, even to the most talented people. Sometimes luck plays a major part in a person's career. Sometimes the "look" will make or break your career. If you are not flexible enough to seek other roles that are suited to you, you may have difficulty landing the roles you want. If you persevere, have faith in your talent, and are willing to be patient and flexible, you can be counted as a working actor—if not an out-and-out star.

Directors

If you become an actor, you inevitably will work with a director. But what do directors do? Do you really need them? As much as you might think that an actor has to be the only one who can adequately interpret a role, directors see and interpret the whole play with all its characters, situations, and emotions. Therefore, they are in charge of selecting the cast, calling rehearsal times, and leading the cast and crew through to the final production.

Directors have to oversee the whole production and even approve all costumes, set design and music. They may have to soothe an actor's ego when their directions clash with the actor's interpretation of the role.

They also have to work under the stress of a budget and schedule and are responsible for all personnel problems. Each actor has to develop an individual role, and all actors have to be able to work as team members in order for the production to run smoothly.

Education and Training

Although directors do not have rigid educational and training requirements, the path to the theater could be very similar to the path for actors. That is, the director should have a broad liberal arts background, with concentration in drama, directing, writing plays, stage movement, speech, and history of the theater. Business courses are also helpful.

Getting Started

You may start out at small, local theaters and, as your reputation grows, you could advance to larger productions in major cities. You may work in movies and television, as well as in the theater.

Because of the demand for American productions throughout the world and the increase in the number of cable television stations, career prospects look good for directors, as well as for actors. The crossover between media and entertainment will contribute to new and more numerous career possibilities. And since people continue to attend the theater—and if you prefer performing live—you can also have a good career as an actor or director in the theater.

Earnings

Just as actors and extras belong to unions that negotiate hours, salaries, and other working conditions, directors also have unions. Those who work in the theater join the Society of Stage

Directors and Choreographers. Those who work in television and film join the Directors Guild of America.

Recent salary figures for a five-week rehearsal period on Broadway amount to about $12,000. Smaller theaters offer between $525 and about $2,300 per week. These smaller theaters, however, may offer you many more opportunities for employment.

Dancers

Some of the most spectacular performing artists that everyone loves to watch are dancers. Whether it is the ballet, modern, jazz, folk, or those dances that are performed in musicals, operettas, or operas, these professionals dazzle us with their fancy footwork, spectacular costumes, and incredible leaps, pirouettes, whirls, and twirls.

Whether they dance solo or with a group, dancers often leave us breathless with the power and grace of their movements and their seemingly effortless defiance of gravity. This must be the closest thing to flying with the birds that most humans ever achieve. And how beautiful it is to watch!

Training and Education

What does it take to fly with the birds? Or just to leap with grace and precision? Most dancers have to start training when they are still children. According to the American Guild of Musical Artists (AGMA), girls can begin formal ballet training between eight and 12 years of age. Boys can begin this training between 12 and 16 years old. AGMA also recommends basic ballet techniques for all dancers, including modern, jazz, and tap. AGMA reports that you can find good dance schools in *Dance Magazine,* in your phone book, or in other publications focused on dance.

By the time you are a teenager, your dance teacher will know whether you have the body type and the potential to continue with the kind of intensive training that would lead to a professional dance career. If you are training for the ballet, this would be the time to begin concentrated training at a ballet school. Some of the major dance school companies may offer summer training programs that could lead to your being admitted to their year-round training programs.

The key to success in ballet is practice, practice, practice—that is what you should be doing in your early and mid-teen years. In your late teens, you will begin your first professional auditions.

Other dancers have to be just as dedicated as ballet dancers. Their bodies and minds have to be disciplined; they must train, practice, and audition just like the ballerinas. Their training may not last as long as that for ballet dancers, however.

A career in dance does not necessarily require a college degree. In fact, because of all the time you must devote to training and practice, your academic life after high school may be a little sporadic. Still, some specialists recommend that you receive as broad an education as possible.

One thing you might want to keep in mind is that your career as a dancer may only last 12 to 15 years, according to AGMA. Therefore, you may want to think about preparing for a second career while you are still young. That may include getting a four-year degree which would allow you to become a dance teacher or choreographer when your active career as a dancer comes to an end.

Some colleges and universities do offer degrees in dance. If you decide not to attend the full four years, however, courses in music, literature, history of the dance, and even acting could be helpful to your career. A dancer, after all, has to interpret roles much as an actor does. Feelings, emotions, and ideas are transmitted to the audience through body movements and facial expressions, and they all have to blend together with the music.

What It Takes

As you might suspect, dancers have to be in top physical form. They also have to be agile, coordinated, creative, persevering, and disciplined. Dancers, like actors, will have to audition and, therefore, will face rejection. Like actors, they also have to follow directions, rehearse long hours, and usually work within a troupe of other dancers. Dancers may also have to face the very real possibility of not being employed all the time. A backup job will be needed as you establish your career as a dancer just as it is for actors.

How to Find Work

When you are ready to audition, check out the listings in *Dance Magazine*, *Backstage*, and *Variety*. After you are a bit more established in your career, word-of-mouth seems to be an effective method for getting auditions.

Another similarity between actors and dancers is that dancers also belong to unions. The American Guild of Musical Artists (AGMA) is the union for ballet, opera, and modern dancers. The American Federation of Television and Radio Artists (AFTRA) is for you if you work in those media. The Screen Actors Guild (SAG) and Screen Extras Guild (SEG) will be your movie unions, and Actors' Equity Association is for dancers who work in musical comedies.

How hard is it to become a working dancer? In some ways, it depends on how dedicated you are to your training and practice. Luck also plays a part in your career because in all the performing arts, the competition for jobs is high. There are always more people auditioning for any performance than there are roles to fill. And since the major hubs for these jobs are New York and Hollywood, most artists flock to these cities, where the competition for jobs becomes even more intense.

This is where your perseverance and faith in yourself become crucial. Remember that not everyone becomes a Barishnikov or an Astaire, but you can develop, with patience and practice, a good night-owl career in dance.

Another similarity with actors is that your initial salary may not be very big because you may not be working steadily as a dancer. You will probably have to supplement your dancing jobs with temporary office work, waiting on tables, or some dance-related job, if possible.

Your union will negotiate your contract with the producer of the show. Your contract may provide paid sick leave and vacations and possibly some health insurance. One recent salary figure for first-year dancers in a single performance was $230, with $60 an hour for rehearsals. Dancers on a one hour television show are paid $569 for the show. Dancers are paid more while on tour.

So even though your salary may not fly with the birds, your dedication to your art, whether you are a ballet, modern, jazz, or tap dancer, will allow you to reach your own personal heights. Training, practice, and patience will be your guide in this dazzling night owl career.

Musicians

Perhaps you feel you lack acting or dancing talent but would love to be performing on the stage, in the movies, or on television. You're taking piano, guitar, saxophone, or singing lessons, and your teacher thinks you have real talent, natural rhythm, and dedication.

You find yourself loving to practice even though all your friends are out playing baseball or going to the movies. You have a great stereo and lots of CDs that you listen to for hours on end. You go to live concerts whenever possible and belong to your school band, have your own combo, or belong to the glee club.

In other words, maybe you can see yourself as a musician or singer up there on that stage, instead of as an actor or dancer. Or possibly you can see yourself conducting an orchestra in some beautiful concert hall in a glamorous European capital.

Well, you are on the right track already because of your lessons, your talent, and your practice. These are just the first few, but important, steps. The Music Educators National Conference (MENC) warns budding musicians that career opportunities are limited and that only those talented people with perseverance and stamina will make it.

What are those opportunities? Musical career opportunities exist in chamber and classical music, folk, rock, pop, and jazz; in combos, trios, and orchestras; in choirs or as solo artists. You could be working in a studio, in a club, at the opera or ballet, in a musical comedy or in a concert hall. You could perform in the movies, on television, or on the radio. Or you could be on tour throughout the world.

The three major categories of musical careers for night owls are instrumentalist, vocalist or singer, and conductor. Let's see which category you might fit into. It may also be possible to be a combination of two or even three of these categories. In other words, you might sing and play an instrument.

Instrumentalists are those who play musical instruments and perform with a band, orchestra, or smaller group. This means any instrument, from a piano to a cello from a drum to a trumpet, or a saxophone to a flute—and all instruments in between. Large musical groups, such as orchestras, will need the full complement of string, wind, percussion, and brass, while a jazz combo may only need a pianist, drummer, and saxophonist.

Singers come in several categories: soprano, mezzo-soprano, contralto, tenor, baritone, and bass. Sopranos and tenors are at the higher end of the voice range, with the contralto and bass as the lowest. Mezzo-sopranos and baritones are the middle-range voices. Your voice range may help you to determine where you will find your career niche. Your personal preference for music will do the rest. This preference will range anywhere from op-era to folk, rock to rhythm and blues, country to rap, and all points in between.

Singers may work with a group in a musical comedy or oper-etta or interpret favorite songs in a personal style as a soloist. It is also possible to cross over successfully from one category of song to another. For example, opera stars, such as Jose Carreras or Placido Domingo, also have performed and recorded songs from the Broadway stage or folk songs native to their own country. Broadway show tunes or romantic ballads can also be interpreted by a jazz instrumentalist or singer to put a whole new twist on them.

Conductors work with orchestras and bands by selecting the musicians and directing all their rehearsals and performances. These professionals must have the ability not only to interpret a whole piece, but also to lead the orchestra through every detail of that interpretation.

Conductors must be diplomatic because individual musicians may have different ideas about interpretation. Most successful conductors also have a dramatic style and stage presence that help them make their mark on the musical world.

Training and Education

For all these careers, you will not necessarily need a college degree, but you need the equivalent in training. You can get that training by studying privately with a master musician, at a conservatory of music, or through regular practice with a band or combo. Colleges and universities also offer degrees in mu-sic. So if you are taking music or singing lessons, you are off to the right start. For all these careers, you will, however, need a high school diploma.

What It Takes

The Music Educators National Conference (MENC) has set up certain guidelines for each of these career choices that will help to guide you through your career in music. Then you can take a look at yourself and your talent and ambition to see where you fit in.

For example, as an instrumentalist, you will have to be able to work well with others and be willing to study continually as well as practice. You will need all this in addition to talent and skill. On top of that, you will have to be able to sight-read, transpose, and improvise music; specialize in at least one instrument; be able to play with other musicians; and be knowledgeable in the literature about your instrument.

Ideally, by the time you have graduated from high school, you will have learned how to read music and have participated in some kind of performance to get used to being on the stage and to prepare yourself for auditions. You might also have performed solo by this time, as well as with the high school band or orchestra or with a small combo.

Singers also need "raw" talent, but they must develop specialized skills depending on the type of songs they choose to sing. Knowledge of English and all its nuances and, for many singers, knowledge of foreign languages will be necessary for a successful career. You will also have to be able to sight read, interpret, and memorize. Some piano playing ability is also an asset. You will have to have some knowledge of vocal literature, be willing to continually study and practice, and have a touch of the showman in you to dramatically interpret an individual song or an entire opera.

Ideally, by the time you have finished high school, you will be able to play rudimentary piano, read music, and have some experience in performing with a group or alone. If your school has a glee club or your church has a choir, join them. The more you sing, the better you will become. And although some singers have been successful without any formal training, you are encouraged to keep up your formal training, especially if you are training for the opera, operetta, or stage shows.

Earnings

According to MENC, you can earn $300 to $1,200 a week as an instrumentalist in an orchestra; $350 to $700 a week in a dance band or night club; and $50 to $4,000 per concert as a member of a small ensemble. Salaries for rock and jazz groups are too wide ranging to estimate or average. Obviously, the bigger the name, the bigger the paycheck, so until you're a Leonard Bernstein or a Whitney Houston, you will definitely work irregularly and for lower fees.

As a vocalist for a dance band or night club, you can earn $225 and up per week. If you are a member of a professional opera company, you will earn at least $350 to $750 a week, and as an opera soloist, you can earn from $350 to $8,000 per performance.

Dance band conductors earn from $300 to $1,200 a week; opera and choral group conductors, $8,000 or more. Symphony conductors' salaries vary so much that they are too difficult to average.

How to Find Work

The American Federation of Musicians of the United States and Canada (AFM), the world's largest union for performing artists, has some tips for aspiring musicians on how to break into the business. This group knows that you have invested a great deal of time and money in lessons, instruments, and maybe even costumes and stage equipment. Now you want to pursue a career with your talent.

According to AFM, you have to start out by talking to people who are already in the business. Find out where the jobs are, how musicians are treated at certain clubs or lounges, and who are the best agents and managers. These agents and managers are responsible for promoting you and eventually getting you jobs, or gigs, as they're called in the music world.

Because the music business is growing rapidly, there are a lot of people competing for the same jobs. The big jobs are again in New York and Los Angeles, as well as other major cities. For country music, you might head for Nashville or Branson. Dixieland jazz is at its best in New Orleans, and small jazz and rock clubs are found everywhere.

It is important for beginning musicians to protect themselves from unethical agents and managers. For this reason, musicians as well as actors and dancers often join unions or professional membership organizations. They include AFM, AGMA, and the American Symphony Orchestra League. The National Association of Schools of Music is the accrediting association for post-secondary musical education programs, and MENC supplies career information. All these organizations are set up to guide, protect, and encourage professional musicians through a long and rewarding career in the musical field of their choice. And, as we all know, life without music is no life at all.

Behind the Scenes

Not all the people in the entertainment industry are visible, but they are absolutely necessary to our enjoyment of the various performers. These are the stagehands, carpenters, makeup artists, hair stylists, costumers, electricians, set designers, and property handlers.

Among the night owls who are not in the movies but who bring them to us are the projectionists, box office attendants, and concession attendants. You may want to make a career of these jobs, or you may be able to take these jobs as you pursue your dancing, acting, or musical careers.

Projectionists perform many duties, especially if they have to operate more than one projector. In the new multi-screen theaters, for example, projectionists often have to operate from 10 to 12 projectors at the same time.

The projectionists' basic responsibilities include removing the 35mm film from the reel in sequence and loading it onto the "platter," which is a film transport system. Then they have to thread the film onto the projector by hand, which requires dexterity and precision because the film has to be aligned carefully. You'll have to be able to move quickly from projector to projector, with a distance of sometimes 75 feet between them. Projectionists have to maintain the projection booth and all the equipment and often have to make small repairs or adjustments, such as splicing film breaks. Projectionists don't need a college degree, but they do have to be physically fit, have good eyesight and hearing, and enjoy working alone.

Concession attendants work at night to be sure that we have enough food and beverages to get us through the performance. At movie theaters, attendants serve food and beverages shortly before the movie begins, but for stage performances and the opera, food and beverages are consumed during the intermissions.

Concession attendants assist in stocking supplies, maintaining the work area, operating cooking and popping machines, and sometimes hauling bulk food items from storage to the work area.

Box office attendants sell tickets, answer customer questions about performance times and prices, and describe show content, if necessary. They also help the manager count cash and keep records. Sometimes they double as doorkeepers or ushers.

Theater managers, ushers, and doorkeepers round out the night owls who open the doors and keep the theaters and movie houses running smoothly so that we can enjoy the wonderful performances of the artists on stage or on film.

Profile of a Musician

John Brumbach, jazz saxophonist with the Chicago Boogie Ensemble, did not exactly come from a musical family, although his father dabbled with the piano and his mother loved records of Frank Sinatra and Broadway musicals, such as *Oklahoma* and *My Fair Lady*. John himself started taking piano lessons when he was about eight years old, but he characterizes his teacher as a "third-rate hack." He played for weddings and graduation parties in hotels and, according to John, didn't "know where it was at" with music. He also took clarinet lessons for about a year but couldn't wait to get out of that class.

During his high school years, John didn't pursue music very seriously, but he remembers loving Elvis Presley and his sound. He also had a brief fling with a rhythm and blues band in his basement. All in all, his musical background at this stage did not point to his later success with the saxophone.

During high school, John ran into a recurring problem in his life that he eventually overcame and which may have actually led him back to his real addiction: music. That problem was drug and alcohol abuse. The problem followed him for years, in and out of musical attempts and actual successful career opportunities. John wants to make it clear to any aspiring musician that the demon was within *him*—it had nothing to do with pursuing a musical career or associating with musicians. In fact, the musicians he plays with now lead a clean and sober life, and that helps him to keep on the straight and narrow path, too.

It took John a few years to realize what his true path in life was. In college, he experienced severe problems from the drug abuse. He became paranoid and nervous all the time. Unfortunately, by his second or third semester in college, John was incapable of doing academic work. He was very good at math and found it easy and enjoyable, but by that time nothing worked for him.

Somehow, almost intuitively, John knew that music could act in a therapeutic way for him. He dropped out of the University of Illinois, borrowed some money from his brother to buy a horn, and started to hang out with musicians. At that time, too, he loved listening to records of the soulful sax soloist King Curtis and the Queen of Soul, Aretha Franklin.

John also picked up some exercise books and just started playing intensely. He admits that the only time he felt okay was when he was playing. He was living in a rooming house and playing about eight hours a day. This was his training for becoming a successful professional jazz saxophonist. Just as a writer has to write, and a dancer has to dance, a musician has to play—and sometimes that intensive playing becomes the musician's formal education.

During that time, John was playing the blues with his brother, and he truly thought he had found the answer for his life and the solution to his problems: music. But his addictions came back to haunt him again in Los Angeles, where he was beginning to explore new career possibilities. He lost his career and his wife there, as a result of drug and alcohol abuse, and decided to return to Chicago.

After about two years playing in honky tonks, John had the good fortune to start playing with master jazz pianist Erwin Helfer at Andy's, a jazz institution in Chicago. John is a talented man in two fields and had been working during the day as an engineer. That job was beginning to stress him out, and he was also realizing how important music was to him. It was time to make a decision that would affect him and his family for the rest of his life.

John decided to return full time to music, both performing and teaching. But his engineering company offered him part-time work, which he accepted. This has worked out well for John, who now works 1 to 2 days a week as an engineer and has made a full-time commitment to music.

His private students range in age from nine to 40 years old, although he did once have a 65-year-old student. He currently teaches eight adults and four children.

Even with the part-time engineering job and the private tutorials, John still has time to practice. He has built a soundproof practice room in his attic for that purpose. This is what he calls his "woodshedding" time—the time when he practices alone.

John is a firm believer in practice; he thinks it makes a musician grow. Through practice, he stays excited and committed and continues to learn about himself. But he thinks that teaching music helps him to articulate what he knows intuitively.

John admits that there was a time in his life when he downplayed the technical aspect of his art. He now knows that it is extremely important and leads to more creative aspects of playing. The ease of performing comes from knowing the technical aspects of the music and your instrument so well that all the time and effort you put into it will pay off in the performance itself.

In performance, John says, you will hardly know that you have a horn in your hand. All your musical expression will go "from the center of your being out into the center of the universe." John thinks that when you are playing with inspired and sensitive musicians, it is a spiritual and mental experience, an act of selflessness. For John, it is the greatest "high" he will ever want to achieve. That is when his technical and creative skills merge into an experience far more powerful than drugs. John is happy to be doing what he is doing and plans to be a musician for a long time.

Since John works at night, however, he admits it's hard on family life. His wife works normal hours, but he does have her support for his career choice. He loves not having to fight rush-hour traffic, and shopping is easier during the day. He also enjoys conversing with his regular customers at Andy's, and he feels that he's a more valuable employee because he knows them.

John advises anyone who wants to be a professional musician to first of all follow your heart. He emphasizes that you have to look out for yourself financially, but he cautions against going into music for the money. He thinks you should find positive and creative people, especially teachers, and to avoid hacks. Musicians should be musicians out of love, pure and simple. Seek out others who are passionate about music as early as you can.

John also thinks that, although you really don't have to go to college to be a musician, education enhances everyone's life. It doesn't hurt to take business courses in college as well as music because you will have to negotiate contracts, work with agents, and manage your money. You should also play as often as possible, even if it's in your basement or garage, alone or with a group. Be with musicians, learn from them, and play with them. That way, you'll have the beginnings of a truly rewarding career with music, no matter what the hours are.

For Further Information

Actors' Equity Association
165 West 46th St.
New York, NY 10036

American Arts Alliance
1319 F St., NW
Suite 307
Washington, DC 20004

American Council for the Arts
1285 Ave. of the Americas
Third Floor
New York, NY 10019

American Dance Guild
33 West 21st St.
Third Floor
New York, NY 10010

American Federation of Musicians of the United States and
Canada
Paramount Building
1501 Broadway
Suite 600
New York, NY 10036

American Guild of Musical Artists (AGMA)
1727 Broadway
New York, NY 10019

American Guild of Organists
815 Second Ave.
Suite 318
New York, NY 10017

American Music Conference
303 East Wacker Dr.
Suite 1314
Chicago, IL 60601

American Symphony Orchestra League
777 Fourteenth St., NW
Suite 500
Washington, DC 20005

American Theatre Association
1010 Wisconsin Ave., NW
Washington, DC 20007

Associated Actors and Artists of America
165 West 46th St.
New York, NY 10036

Association of Canadian Orchestras
56 The Esplanade
Suite 311
Toronto, Ontario, Canada M5E lA7

Association of College, University and Community Arts
Administrators, Inc.
1112 16th St., NW
Suite 620
Washington, DC 20036

Broadcast Music, Inc.
320 West 57th St.
New York, NY 10019

Center for Arts Information
1285 Ave. of the Americas
Third Floor
New York, NY 10019

The College Music Society
1444 Fifteenth St.
Boulder, CO 80302

Conductors' Guild, Inc.
P.O. Box 3361
West Chester, PA 19381

International Alliance of Theatrical Stage Employees and
Moving Picture Machine Operators of the United States and
Canada (I.A.T.S.E.).)
1515 Broadway
Suite 601
New York, NY 10036

International Society for Music Education
14 Bedford Square
London, England WCIB 3JC

J.F. Kennedy Center for the Performing Arts
Internship Coordinator
Alliance for Arts Education
Washington, DC 20566

Music Educators National Conference (MENC)
1902 Association Dr.
Reston, VA 22091

Music Teachers National Association
617 Vine St.
Suite 1432
Cincinnati, OH 45202

National Association of Schools of Music (NASM)
11250 Roger Bacon Dr.
Suite 21
Reston, VA 22090
NASM publications:
  Assessment of Community Programs in Music
  Assessment of Undergraduate Programs in Music
  Assessment of Graduate Programs in Music
  Community Education and Music Programs in Higher Education
  Monographs on Music in Higher Education Directory

National Association of Theatre Owners
4605 Lankershim Blvd.
Suite 340
North Hollywood, CA 91602-1891
Publication:
  Careers in the Motion Picture Industry

National Endowment for the Arts
Fellowship Program
1100 Pennsylvania Ave., NW
Washington, DC 20506

The National Music Council
45 West 34th St.
Suite 1010
New York, NY 10001

National School Orchestra Association
39 East 200 South
Smithfield, UT 84335

Opportunity Resources for the Arts
1457 Broadway
New York, NY 10036

CHAPTER SEVEN

Security and Social Services

Night Owls Who Serve the Public

Of all the careers that we have discussed so far, none is as important to our safety and well being as the law enforcement officer on the beat, the fire fighter protecting our homes, or the security guard where we work at night. We can't forget the dispatcher who makes sure that the vital emergency services are delivered in a timely fashion.

Other night owls who make sure that the cables, electric power, and utilities function 24 hours a day are the line installers and cable splicers. Still others help us get through the night by providing counseling for drug abuse, domestic violence, or runaway children. Without these dedicated professionals, our lives would be without the safety net that we all need when we are in trouble.

Law Enforcement

Most of us see police officers every day on our way to school or work. They may be patrolling the streets in cars, on foot, on a motorcycle, or on a horse. They could be directing traffic at busy intersections or chasing a car down the street with sirens blaring and flashing lights on.

They may even be pulling us over to give us a ticket for speeding. Unfortunately, they may also just get to the parking meter a minute before we do and be writing up a parking ticket for us. Sometimes we might have to call them for help with prowlers or burglars. We may also see them at the scene of a fire, accident, or expressway tie-up.

Law enforcement officers also work behind the scene. There are, for example, detectives, special agents, and experts in chemical analysis and fingerprint identification. In smaller towns, where there is no official police department, you might find town or county sheriffs. In addition, every state has its own police squad, also called state troopers.

The federal government has a special investigative department known as the Federal Bureau of Investigation, more commonly known as the FBI. Still other federal law enforcement agents work for the Department of Treasury, while Secret Service agents protect the president and other top federal officials and their families.

Law enforcement personnel are just as concerned with the prevention of crime as they are with solving crimes and arresting the criminals. Municipal police officers are becoming more and more involved in community work and are trying to be more responsive to the needs of the particular community. In some cases, drugs and gangs are the biggest problem. In others, burglaries and petty larceny need the most attention. An effective police department will be aware of the specific problems and population it is dealing with.

Detectives aren't as noticeable as the "cops on the beat" because they work in civilian clothes, but they are there helping investigate crimes, gather evidence, and conduct on-site interviews with victims and witnesses to crime.

Agents in the FBI are charged with investigating specific federal crimes, including organized crime, espionage, kidnapping, sabotage, and terrorism. They may also specialize in such financial crimes as embezzlement or counterfeiting. Other federal agents work for the Customs Service and the Internal Revenue Service.

State troopers are found mainly on intrastate highways, patrolling for lawbreakers and assisting drivers in trouble. They also are found at accident or disaster scenes, where they clear traffic and see that victims are taken care of. If you ever have car trouble on the highway, they will be there to give you assistance. Sometimes state troopers are called upon to help solve crimes, especially where there is no local police department.

What It Takes

Wherever you work as a law enforcement officer, you will have to have certain characteristics and personal qualities. You must be honest and responsible and have a real need to help people. Since you are involved on a daily basis with people in trouble or in stress, you will have to think quickly, demonstrate fairness, and exercise good judgment.

In many cases, before you become a law enforcement officer or federal agent, you may have to be tested for your psychological stability, use of drugs, and honesty. You may be required to take a lie detector test and undergo a background check.

Training and Education

How do you get into law enforcement? Some police departments offer high school graduates a police cadet or trainee program. These teenagers who are interested in becoming police officers serve as clerks while they attend classes, becoming officers at age 21 if they fulfill all the requirements.

As with many employers, police departments and law enforcement agencies want people with at least a high school diploma. More and more cities and states are, however, requiring some college work if not a degree from a college or university. Community colleges offer courses in law enforcement, but no matter where you attend, certain courses are recommended. These courses include English, American history, psychology, business law, and sociology.

Your communications skills, especially in English, are extremely important because you will have to write reports and verbally transmit directions to a wide variety of people to ensure their safety. You will also be called on occasionally to testify in court. Because Spanish is spoken by so many people in the United States, some knowledge of it is very helpful.

As a law enforcement officer, you will have to be a U.S. citizen and at least 20 years old. In addition to your academic credentials, you will have to be in top physical condition because you will undergo strict physical examinations, including vision testing.

Before you become a police officer, you will have to undergo certain training. The length of time will vary from location to location but will usually include some classroom instruction that will emphasize constitutional and state law, civil ordinances, and civil rights laws. In addition, you will learn about the use of firearms, self-defense, and traffic control.

Where You Start

After your training, you will probably start out on patrol. During this time, you will work with a more experienced officer in different areas of your beat. You will have to be on the lookout for anything unusual, suspicious, or dangerous. You might even have to respond to actual calls. You will keep in constant contact with headquarters throughout your shift.

After a certain period as a beat officer or patrol officer, which varies from department to department, you may be eligible for promotion, usually to detective. Or, you may decide to specialize in a specific area, such as traffic or communications. In order to be promoted up the line, that is from sergeant to lieutenant to captain, you will have to pass a written examination which will be evaluated with your performance to that point.

To apply for a job as an FBI agent, you will need to have a college degree in either accounting, engineering, or computers; be a law school graduate; or speak, read, and write a foreign language fluently. If you don't have the degree or language fluency, you must have worked full time for at least three years. You must be a U.S. citizen between 23 and 35 years old and willing to relocate. You must be physically fit and have good, though perhaps corrected, vision. If you are accepted, you will receive your training at the FBI academy in Virginia.

If you want to work for the Treasury Department as a special agent, you will need a college degree and at least three years of work experience, with two of them involving criminal investigation, or a combination of the two. You'll have to be at least 35 years old and complete 16 weeks of training.

Job Prospects and Earnings

Your job prospects are good in the next few years if you decide to become a law enforcement officer or special agent. Those who have a bachelor's degree or have received some college training will receive the best jobs. Salaries, benefits, and opportunities for advancement are quite good in this field, and many police officers can retire rather young and receive a good pension. Often you will also be able to earn overtime pay, and your benefits will probably include paid vacations and sick days, as well as medical and life insurance.

Salaries will vary according to whether you are working for a city, state, or federal agency, or whether you work in a big city or small town. However, recent surveys suggest $22,400 as the average salary for an entry-level police officer, $28,300 for FBI agents, and between $17,000 and $21,000 for Treasury agents.

What to Expect

Now, if you think that law enforcement work is for you, you have to realize that you will be on call 24 hours a day. You will have to be prepared to work different shifts and to give up weekends and holidays. But if you think you have what it takes, the night owl in you will overcome these obstacles.

Interview with a Campus Police Officer

Ron Ervin has been a police officer on the Purdue University/ Calumet extension campus in Hammond, Indiana, for the past seven years. As such, he is very familiar with shift work. He works now on a four-week rotating shift, which he likes pretty well. Every four weeks it changes from 7 A.M. to 3 P.M., 3 P.M. to 11 P.M., and 11 P.M. to 7 A.M. He feels this is a much easier schedule to adjust to than a one-week rotation, especially when it comes to eating and sleeping habits. He also has an easier time in planning his weekends and vacations.

He developed his interest in law enforcement in the eighth grade, and it has never left him. Because he came from a broken home and then lost both his parents, he wanted to turn this pain into doing something worthwhile with his life.

Ron found encouragement from one of his teachers and also from some police officers he knew at the time. He even got involved in a local ride-along program, which allowed high school students to participate in certain police activities.

Ron graduated from high school when he was only 17, and no police department would hire him at that age. He then decided to join the United States Marine Corps for four years. And—you guessed it—he was an MP (military police). He received valuable on-the-job training and was in charge of his company's armory, which allowed him to learn a great deal about firearms.

When Ron left the service, he applied at Purdue's North Central extension campus and was hired. At that time he received one year of basic training, including a 10-week course at the police academy. His time at the academy was devoted to studying criminal law, first aid, traffic accidents, domestic disputes, and riot control. Sometimes lifelike scenarios were set up by the more experienced officers to see how the cadets would react to them.

He thinks that the graveyard shift is difficult, but challenging. He is the only officer on duty at that time, and he really likes that feeling of independence. Sometimes the campus is quiet, especially during the summer when there are very few students. At about 4 A.M., he begins to get tired and he has no one to talk to, except maybe the custodial staff in buildings he patrols. He often drinks a lot of coffee and depends on the radio for company.

Ron doesn't just patrol the campus, though. The campus police department has a mutual assistance program with the Hammond police department, so he patrols the immediate community, too. If he sees anything suspicious, such as a burglary in progress, he radios the Hammond police, who come and provide assistance. This whole program gives everyone on campus and in the surrounding community a better sense of security.

Some people whom he stops for a traffic offense or parking problem really don't believe that he is a genuine police officer because he works on campus. They think he is a security guard and only believe him when they meet in court.

Besides the independence, he loves on the graveyard shift, Ron loves the challenge of knowing that no two calls are ever the same. Sometimes he's called for a family dispute, a barroom brawl, or a foot pursuit. Sometimes he redirects kids who are just out wandering after curfew.

On weekends, there are usually more alcohol-related incidents than on week nights, especially right after the bars close.

There is always more danger at night simply because you can't always see it coming. But that edge can make your blood run, and you are suddenly wide awake.

Ron thinks that it's a good idea to get an associate's degree if you want to become a police officer, but a bachelor's degree would be even better. That degree will be a must for everyone in the near future. Typical courses to take are criminology, computer science, and English. If you decide to take a foreign language, it should be Spanish.

Many police cars are now equipped with computers that allow officers to check license plates, drivers' licenses, stolen cars, or pending calls. This new technological capability seems to be effective in deterring crime because would-be criminals are becoming aware that patrol cars arrive on the scene much faster now.

Ron emphasizes grammar, spelling, writing, and verbal skills. You have to be able to talk to a wide variety of people, no matter which shift you're working. You will write up many official reports, which the judge and the defense and prosecuting attorneys have to read. These are legal documents and are also reflections on your department. If you are a poor speller, at least learn how to use your dictionary.

Ron suggests that you ask your local police department whether they sponsor ride-along programs for young people. Some state police departments also offer summer camps to familiarize students with police work. Get to know your local law enforcement officers. Talk to them about their jobs and see whether they might recommend books to read about the work.

Would Ron recommend this work? Without hesitation. It is very challenging, and you are in a position to do something good for other people. That's what he has had in mind since eighth grade.

Fire Fighters

Another equally important career for those of you who are not only night owls but also want to help people in trouble is that of fire fighter. These professionals not only put out fires, they also try to prevent fires from starting by inspecting buildings and their fire escapes and by checking for any dangerous and flammable materials on the premises. Fire fighters also work with schools and community groups to instruct them on fire-prevention techniques, the use of smoke detectors, and how to react to a fire.

When a fire occurs, wherever it occurs, the fire fighters' primary duty is to put it out as quickly and efficiently as possible with as little damage or loss of life as possible. At the scene of the fire, they may have to perform a variety of duties, including giving first aid, operating heavy equipment, and working with emergency medical technicians.

When they're not on the scene of a fire, they spend their time at the fire station, probably working more than the standard 40-hour work week. At the station, they help maintain the equipment, write up reports, and sometimes attend training sessions. They need to keep up with current literature in the field. They sleep and eat at the station, too, because of the demands of shift rotations.

What to Expect

Fire fighters work different shifts, generally more than 40 hours a week. They may work a straight 24 hours and be off for 48 hours. Or, they might work the day shift for a couple of weeks and then night shift for a couple of weeks. The shifts will vary from place to place, and fire fighters are on call at any time during the shift.

Fire fighting is dangerous, often grueling work. Fire fighters are exposed to flames, smoke, hazardous chemicals, toppling buildings, and caved-in walls. They perform their work outdoors in all possible weather conditions. They assist in rescuing victims of tornadoes, hurricanes, floods, and other natural disasters as well as human-caused accidents such as oil spills or chemical explosions.

Because fire fighters work under pressure, they have to exercise good judgment in emergency situations, make immediate decisions to ensure safety, and be physically strong. A fire fighter has to be able to wake up from a sound sleep and instantly be ready to respond to a dangerous situation.

As a member of a team that lives and works together, fire fighters must be able to get along well with other people. This kind of teamwork demands reliability, flexibility, and a good sense of humor. So, if you're still interested in becoming a fire fighter, let's look at what it will take.

Training and Education

To become a fire fighter you will need at least a high school diploma or its equivalent and be at least 18 years old. Then you must pass a written exam, a medical exam, and tests of physical strength, stamina, and coordination. A drug test may also be required. Those with the highest scores on all exams—and a negative drug test—will be admitted to a training program. If you've served as an apprentice or intern at a fire department or had experience as a volunteer fire fighter, you will probably have a better chance of being a successful candidate.

Then you will be trained in class for a few weeks in such subjects as fire fighting techniques, building codes, fire prevention, and appropriate medical procedures. You will learn how to use your equipment, including ladders, axes, and extinguishers. After the training period, you will finally be assigned to your fire station. But you're still on probation, and you're really just beginning to learn.

Because of the increasing responsibilities of fire fighters and the more sophisticated equipment and technology involved in fire fighting, fire fighters must continually update their knowledge in techniques and procedures. This continuing education is especially necessary if you want to be promoted.

Many colleges now offer degrees in fire science. They can be acquired in two to four years, and tuition costs are sometimes reimbursed by the fire department. You might inquire in advance whether your station encourages continuing education through a tuition reimbursement plan.

Sometimes the department itself offers additional training programs for its employees, and some states also have such programs. If you decide to pursue your education, you will probably want to take courses in management, budgeting, advanced equipment, writing, and public speaking.

Promotion within the department is possible after a few years. The usual progression is from captain to battalion chief to assistant chief to deputy chief and all the way to chief. You'll have to pass a written exam to be considered for promotion. Then your superiors will factor in your previous performance on the job and the number of years you have served. More and more fire departments also require advanced degrees for promotion to chief.

Like police officers, fire fighters receive good pay, benefits, and pension plans. Overtime is available after 53 hours in any work period, and most departments provide protective clothing and dress uniforms.

Fire fighters may find entry-level employment possibilities in smaller communities that need more full-time fire fighters to supplement the volunteer force. Salaries vary from region to region and city to city, but a recent survey found $19,700 to be the average annual salary for entry-level positions. As you are promoted or gain experience, your salary will increase.

Security Services

If fire fighting or law enforcement isn't your choice for keeping people safe, perhaps you would like to become a security guard. These people keep watch over our offices, department stores, banks, and hospitals through patrols and inspections of the property. They watch for things like fire, suspicious activity, and vandalism. They often work with department store detectives to catch customers or employees stealing merchandise.

Or you might be assigned to a museum, a laboratory, or a military base where you would guard art objects, formulas, or secret files. Parks and sports facilities also hire guards to check incoming and outgoing personnel and vehicles. They assist customers by answering questions, giving directions, explaining the facility, and directing traffic. Some people hire guards to protect them or their families from harm or kidnapping—hence the name bodyguard. Some guards also deliver large sums of money in armored cars from one place of business to another.

Depending on where you work, you will be patrolling on foot, by car, or even on a motor scooter. You'll have to check out the offices, doors, and windows, as well as any unauthorized people in the building. You may even have to check the heating and sprinkling systems.

Sometimes you will be able to check all this out from your workstation with the help of television monitors. This occurs when cameras are placed in strategic areas of the building so that they "patrol" for you.

And if you're not a clothes horse, you won't mind wearing a uniform. Most guards do, and they also carry a flashlight and a two-way radio. Sometimes they carry guns even though they probably rarely have to use them.

Many times the work is routine, but guards have to be ready for anything. Very often guards who work at night will work alone. Many organizations now require guards 24 hours a day, seven days a week, 365 days a year. In this case, guards may work on rotating shifts. And, yes, guards have to work weekends and holidays.

What It Takes

How do you become a guard? It's best if you have a high school diploma. If you don't have that or its equivalent, you will probably be required to show that you can read and write and can follow written and oral instructions. If you have to drive a vehicle on patrol, you will also need a valid driver's license.

If you have had previous military experience or were a police officer, you will be valuable to employers. And since law enforcement officers can retire fairly early, they often become guards after retirement. The varying shifts also attract people to guard work.

Whether you choose to be a security guard as a first or second career, you have to be in good health and have no police record. Your emotional life has to stable, and you must be reliable and dependable, and physically fit. You may also be required to take lie detector and drug tests.

If you work for a contract security agency, you will have to be licensed. For this, you must be at least 18 years old, have no convictions for perjury or violent crimes, and pass a background check. You will also have to take instruction in property rights and emergency procedures, among other topics.

Training and Education

After you've been hired, you will probably receive on-the-job training. This training might include public relations, protection, report writing, and first aid. You might also learn about firearms or more about the facility you will be guarding. You will also learn about electronic surveillance techniques.

If you want to advance in the security business, you may have to consider further education. For example, some related college courses may make administrative positions possible. If you have management skills, you may want to open your own business.

Employment Expectations and Earnings

Because more businesses are concerned with security and there is relatively high turnover, there should be plenty of jobs available in this field in the near future. Salaries vary from region to region and from facility to facility. The more experience you accumulate, the more you will earn. Guards hired by their own organizations instead of through an agency usually earn more. They also usually get better benefits and have more job security. Guards working in the Midwest generally earn more than those in other areas of the country. Those in the South earn the least.

Dispatchers

If security guard work is not for you, you might want to consider becoming a dispatcher. These are the people who receive calls for help and coordinate all services to solve the problem. Basically there are seven different types of dispatchers:

1. Public safety dispatchers work for police and fire departments and ambulance services. Generally they are part of the 911 system that takes emergency calls, asks pertinent questions regarding the nature of the emergency, finds out the location of the emergency, and decides on appropriate action. If it is a medical case, dispatchers keep talking to the caller in order to give any necessary first aid advice or to find out exact details of the emergency. They are also in contact with the paramedics to get updated information on the patient's

condition.

2. Truck dispatchers work with drivers and customers to expedite delivery, assign drivers, and provide scheduling information.

3. Bus dispatchers keep buses on schedule, both local and long-distance.

4. Train dispatchers see to it that trains arrive and depart on time.

5. Taxi dispatchers inform cab drivers when and where a cab is needed. They also keep records of any road service calls.

6. Tow truck dispatchers take calls for emergency road service and make sure that a tow truck is sent to the site.

7. Gas and water service dispatchers send out emergency crews if gas or water mains break down.

Part of each job entails keeping records, writing reports, and recording the action taken in each situation. Sometimes entries are made directly into a computer. For all these jobs, oral and written communications skills must be very good, and because more and more computers are being used in dispatching, these skills are essential.

The job outlook is fairly promising for dispatching because there is a rather high degree of turnover in this field. This is a high-pressure job, and some people leave it after a few years.

Wire Technicians

Other professionals who look after vital areas of our lives are line installers and cable splicers. These people install power and telephone lines and television cables. They also are on call 24 hours a day to repair them. They work outside in all weather conditions until service is restored or any danger has passed.

Training and Education

Most employers require a high school diploma. Some may also give you a test of basic language and math skills; others may test your strength and coordination, mechanical aptitude, and understanding of the principles of electricity. You may have to take part in an apprenticeship program if you work for an electric company. Telephone workers also have to receive thorough instruction and training to do their jobs.

Some employers now use videocassettes for training purposes, while others set up facilities with poles and other fixtures which simulate actual working conditions. For more formal training, you might be required to take courses in blueprint reading, electrical codes, and electrical theory. Training varies according to whether you are working with telephone, cable television, or electric power companies.

What to Expect

Because of developing technologies with fiber optic cables, satellites, and microwave towers, these jobs may not grow much in the near future. Salaries vary too much even to quote them, but it is a good idea to join a union that will look out for working conditions, salaries, and other benefits.

Social Service Workers

Many people have to work at night to protect our mental and emotional security. These include case workers, drug and alcohol abuse counselors, and residential counselors. They work in group residences, halfway houses, mental health centers, and social service agencies. They help runaway teenagers, battered women and children, and people with psychological problems that they cannot solve themselves.

Many of these professionals work primarily during the day, but they are always on call, including nights and weekends. If they work in group homes, they usually work rotating shifts. Generally they work under the supervision of social workers or sometimes even psychologists.

These professionals provide a wide variety of services, including setting up day-care programs, teaching basic skills, leading recreational activities, and providing transportation to those who need it. They work under pressure because they work with people who have problems that have to be solved, sometimes very quickly.

Training and Education

Although you can get such a job with just a high school diploma, most employers would rather hire people with college training in some branch of the behavioral sciences. Many require a bachelor's degree. You may want to specialize in one or another aspects of social services such as family problems, crisis intervention, drug counseling, or rehabilitation. Or you may decide to work with teenagers, the elderly, or the developmentally disabled. You can get a master's degree in human services and social work to prepare for advancement in this field.

What It Takes

Social workers directly counsel their clients on a wide range of problems including homelessness, illness, drug and alcohol abuse, and child or spouse abuse. They usually specialize in child welfare, family services, mental health, school, community, or clinical social work. Often they have to schedule evening and weekend meetings with their clients, and some are on call at all hours.

All these professionals have to be extremely dedicated, patient, and sensitive to other people and their often severe problems. They have to be dependable, and responsible, as well as emotionally stable. The work is rewarding, especially when successfully solving problems, but since social workers are always dealing with troubled individuals or families, it can be very wearing work.

If you have your master's degree in social work (MSW), you will be able to be able to find work in health care, including mental health care facilities. Or, if you decide to go into administrative or supervisory work, you will need an MSW. A doctorate of social work (DSW) will be needed for teaching and research positions.

Social service workers at all levels are always needed because people are always in need. Police officers, fire fighters, dispatchers, power workers, social service professionals—all of these hard-working professionals make our lives more secure. All these careers are necessary and worthwhile. You just have to want to help people, have the courage and stamina to do it, and get the education to prepare you for other possibilities as a public-service night owl.

For Further Information

American Train Dispatchers Association
1401 South Harlem Ave.
Berwyn, IL 60402

American Trucking Associations, Inc.
2200 Mill Rd.
Alexandria, VA 22314

Associated Public Safety Communications Officers
2040 South Ridgewood
South Daytona, FL 32119

Communications Workers of America
1925 K St., NW
Washington, DC 20006

Contract Guard Information Manual
GPO Publication No. 022-00-00192-2
U.S. Government Printing Office
Washington, DC 20402

Council on Social Work Education
1600 Duke St.
Alexandria, VA 22314

Council for Standards in Human Service Education
Montgomery Community college
340 Dekalb Pike
Blue Bell, PA 19422

International Municipal Signal Association
P.O. Box 539
1115 North Main St.
Newark, NY 14513

National Association of Social Workers
7981 Eastern Ave.
Silver Spring, MD 20910

National Organization for Human Service Education
P.O. Box 6257
Fitchburg State College
Fitchburg, MA 01420

Service Employees International Union
AFL-CIO
1313 L St., NW
Washington, DC 20006

United States Telephone Association
900 19th St., NW
Suite 800
Washington, DC 20006

CHAPTER EIGHT

Other Night Owl Careers

With our topsy-turvy, day-for-night world, it's good to know that certain other services are available to us 24 hours a day. When we run out of milk, baby formula, medicine, or gas in the middle of the night, we are almost always able to find an all-night convenience store, pharmacy, drug store, or gas station.

To get our newspaper in the morning, we need people who are working the printing presses during the night. To eat our Danish or croissant while reading that paper, we depend on bakers who are also night owls. And since some types of businesses are open 24 hours a day, some clerical supervisors and word processing operators are working the night shift. Even some professionals, such as teachers and lawyers, have to work nights. So let's take a look at some of these career possibilities to see if there's a place for another night owl or two.

Sales

This country sometimes seems to be run by salespeople—someone is always selling something somewhere. It may be in a department or grocery store, through the mail, on the radio or television, in magazines or newspapers. There are now even several shopping channels on television that run all day and all night, and computer on-line services allow you to shop on your desktop computer.

Sometimes we buy from farm stands or from flea markets, where everything imaginable can be bought and sold. Kids start selling lemonade at an early age, and entrepreneurs sell their own homemade products to local stores or individual customers. Luckily for all those salespeople, there are enough of us who love to shop till we drop.

Salespeople have to know their product well enough to inform the customer about its special features. They are often responsible for ringing up the sale and packaging the items purchased. Most cash registers are now computerized, so sales personnel must learn that skill.

Those who work at night also probably have to work holidays and weekends. Prompt, efficient service is important for night salespeople because the customer is eager to get home and go to bed.

What It Takes

Even though there are no formal educational requirements for sales, most employers do prefer a high school diploma or equivalent, unless, of course, it is a part time job you work while attending high school. However, certain personal qualities are important for this work.

First of all, you should like dealing with people. This may require a combination of patience, good will, and a healthy sense of humor. Second, your appearance is important because you sometimes serve as the only representative of the store that the customer ever has contact with. Third, courtesy and good oral communication skills are highly important.

Display a positive attitude and a pleasing personality, gain a few years of experience, and you may move up to a supervisory position. If you really want to make a long-term career in retail sales and want to become a middle or top manager, you will probably need a college degree. Some college training coupled with retail experience may land you that executive position.

Regardless of your goal, you will have to start out somewhere, and selling in an all-night convenience, drug, or grocery store is a good start. Part time jobs while you attend high school or college will give you a good idea about whether selling is for you. The customer service skills you learn will put you in a good position for those top-level jobs in your future.

Pharmacists

At many all-night drug stores now there are also many night owl pharmacists. They work through the night for those minor and major medical emergencies that can happen to any of us. We all run out of medicine or need it in a hurry for a sick child or elderly person.

To many people, pharmacists may look as if they simply empty pills into small containers after successfully interpreting the doctor's handwritten prescription. They are really highly trained and licensed professionals who have studied for many years so that they can measure and mix the right drugs and medicines according to the doctor's instructions, as well as provide advice to clients about medications.

Training and Education

Pharmacists study another five years beyond high school in order to receive their Bachelor of Science (B.S.) or Bachelor of Pharmacy (B.Pharm.) degree. A doctorate requires an additional year or two. There are now 74 colleges of pharmacy in this country to choose from.

Some pharmacy schools require you to pass the Pharmacy College Admissions Test (P-CAT), while others require some college pre-pharmacy courses. These include math, chemistry, biology, physics, and social science. Master's and doctoral degree candidates study pharmaceutical chemistry, pharmacology, or pharmacy administration.

In pharmacy college, you will learn how to mix compounds and dispense prescriptions, as well as how to manage your responsibilities as a pharmacist. You will also learn about ethics. After graduation, you obtain a license in order to practice pharmacy. To be licensed, you must pass a state board exam and intern under a licensed pharmacist for a given amount of time, which varies from state to state.

What to Expect

Now what do pharmacists do once they get a job? Since many of the pharmaceutical companies manufacture pre-measured pills, present-day pharmacists spend more time counseling their customers about the use of drugs, determining which medications can safely be taken with others, and learning about the customer's health history. Pharmacists also keep records of medications prescribed to their customers and keep track of all medicines those customers are taking.

In 1990, most pharmacists were working in community pharmacies or in a chain drug, department, or grocery store. If you work in a chain store, you can rise to store manager, supervisory pharmacist, or executive.

Your job outlook as a pharmacist is looking very good in the next few years, partially because of the "graying" of America; that is, more people are middle-aged or elderly in this country than ever before. People in these age ranges usually need more medicines on a consistent basis than younger people. With more and more prescription drugs available and more people using them, your career prospects seem stable through the beginning of the next century.

Earnings

Salaries for pharmacists are also usually quite good. In a recent survey, the average annual base salary for pharmacists in chain stores was $45,800 and in independent drug stores, $41,900. With so much opportunity for the future and with such good earning potential, you might consider becoming a pharmacist and joining other night owls in those all-night stores.

Printers

In a previous chapter, we talked about how reporters, writers, and editors worked though the night to be sure that our morning newspaper is delivered to our homes, put into those boxes on the corner, and distributed to stores and to the vendors on the street. Well, that was just part of the story. Printing press operators are also crucial to our morning reading pleasure

These professionals prepare the presses by installing the printing plate, mixing solutions, fixing the pressure, applying ink, loading the paper and making sure that the paper fits the press. After that, press operators have to monitor the operation, watching to see that the ink is evenly distributed and that the paper doesn't jam. If that happens, the press operator will stop the press and make adjustments.

Press operators may also have to maintain the presses, which for newspapers are usually offset presses. Maintenance consists of cleaning, oiling, and making minor repairs. This is sometimes done with helpers if the press is very large.

Presses for the major newspapers are the large "web" presses that sometimes require several operators and some assistants. The webs are huge rolls of paper that have to be fed into the presses, which then print on both sides of the paper. The press also cuts the papers to size, assembles, and folds them. Since some presses are now at least partially computerized, the press operator often monitors the operation from a control panel.

All of this work requires physical and mental alertness and an ability to fix things quickly. The press room is usually noisy, and operators are generally on their feet almost all the time. There are printing presses everywhere, but job opportunities may be more plentiful in larger cities such as Chicago, New York, Los Angeles, and Washington, D.C.

What It Takes

If this night owl career appeals to you, we'll take a look at what it takes to become a printing press operator. Because technology has entered this field as it has every other, taking courses in chemistry, electronics, color theory, and physics could boost your career opportunities. You will also have to be mechanically inclined, have good oral and written communication skills, and be mathematically proficient.

At any rate, when you start out, you will probably begin at the bottom of the ladder. After being assigned to loading and cleaning the presses, you may start to operate one-color presses and then move up to multi-color operations. It is a good idea to get as much experience on as many presses as possible as you learn your craft and build your career.

Apprenticeship is still available to beginners. It usually consists of on-the-job training under an experienced operator. Sometimes this training is supplemented by classroom instruction or correspondence courses. Any courses that you take in printing will benefit you, and it is important to keep updating your knowledge because of the ever-changing technological advances in the field.

If you are an offset printing operator, your job outlook is good. Even though many major U.S. newspapers have gone under, smaller papers are expected to increase in the coming years. The more experience you have, the more likely your chance of a good career in this business—especially if you are willing to work odd hours.

Bakers

First you have to ask yourself if you like to work in the kitchen. Do you, for example, like to fuss around with different ingredients and come up with something special for guests? Is taste important to you? Can you imagine the satisfaction of a customer who has just tasted one of your delicious donuts? If so, you might turn out to be one of those bakers who toil at night to make sure that we have the donuts, rolls, muffins, breads, and coffee cakes that make waking up worthwhile.

On weekday mornings, we rush to pop a piece of toast into the toaster for a little sustenance to face the day. On weekends, we lazily indulge ourselves in a wonderful brunch with fresh croissants, sweet rolls, English muffins, or hard rolls. We're hooked. We can't face the day without them. And who supplies us with these tasty morsels? The night owl baker does, of course.

The American Institute of Baking (AIB) assures us, however, that bakers don't necessarily prefer night work. The process of refrigeration has enabled bakers to shift back to day work, allowing them a more normal family and social life. Improvements in product formulation and shelf life have also allowed a more normal work week for bakers.

But we have to make a distinction between traditional "craft" bakers and industrial or wholesale bakers, according to the AIB. The craft bakers are those who work nights, earn less money, and work longer hours. But this situation may change because of changing legislation regarding worker safety, sanitation, and employer liability. Until then, you work the graveyard shift.

Whether you are a craft or an industrial baker, your basic job is to mix the proper ingredients according to designated recipes and bake them to specification. In the process, you will have to learn to carefully operate machinery. Trainees can, for instance, now mix, mold, wrap, and slice the bread. Then they may work with people in receiving, warehousing, and shipping to get as much experience in production as possible. As a be-

ginner, though, you will probably start out as a helper or apprentice and then move on to baker and then supervisory positions.

Retail bakers produce their particular goods in large quanti-
ties for sale at grocery stores, hotels, coffee shops, and restaurants. If you are happy with satisfying the various tastes of your
customers and adhering to a professional standard, baking
might be the right night owl career for you.

Training and Education

The AIB is a nonprofit professional organization for those in
the baking profession that promotes education in nutrition, the
science and art of baking, and bakery management. It offers
educational programs, such as the 16-week Baking Science and
Technology and the 10-week Bakery Maintenance Engineering
training programs. Other short courses are offered as well.

The AIB also has research laboratories where nutritional
content is examined and practical solutions are explored to
ensure the highest quality of baked goods. This organization
also oversees sanitation and safety practices and educates baking professionals through in-plant training, correspondence
courses, short courses, training manuals, and audiovisual materials.

The AIB's library staff answers questions from everywhere in
the country and throughout the world. So, if you decide to
become a baker, you will have a professional organization behind you to help you to get the training and education you will
need.

No matter what the state of the economy or the age of the
citizens, bread will always be the staff of life, and we will always
need baked goods to keep us going. So keep practicing in the
kitchen until you get it right, take the courses, and keep us all
happy with your wonderful creations.

Other Night Owl Careers

We have previously talked about professionals, such as doctors and nurses, whom we normally think of as night owls. There are, however, other professionals who also work irregular hours or split shifts and who might need a support staff to get them through the night.

For example, did you know that teachers, librarians, and lawyers often work split shifts, evenings, weekends, holidays, and graveyard shifts? Well, they do. And we'll take a look at how these flexible shifts affect their work.

Lawyers often have to work long hours, well over the normal 40 hours a week. Preparation for a case that is being tried will require working until the job is done, and that often involves overnight work, evenings, holidays, and weekends. Working alongside the lawyers are the paralegals, clerical supervisors, and word processors.

Adult education teachers often work two shifts, such as the morning and evening shift. Others just work weekends, and tutors work at any time that is convenient for their students, including evenings. Librarians and their assistants also work evenings and weekends.

Lawyers

Lawyers represent both defendants and plaintiffs in a court of law, either in civil or criminal cases. They also advise clients as to their legal rights in everyday life and in business. As such, they have to know and interpret the law as it applies to each individual case. This requires a great deal of research regarding the application and purpose of the law.

Lawyers must deal in strictest confidentiality with each client, which is part of their ethical code. They have to write reports or briefs according to their specializations They can specialize in such areas as criminal, corporate, tax, real estate,

probate, or international law. If you want to become a trial lawyer, you will definitely spend long hours in preparation for litigation.

In order to become a lawyer, you will have to complete at
least three years of college and graduate from a law school ap-
proved by the American Bar Association (ABA). Then you
have to pass state bar examination.

In college, you might want to take a liberal arts curriculum,
with emphasis on English, public speaking, economics, computer science, and history. In order to get into law school, you
will have to pass the Law School Admission Test (LSAT), in
addition to having good undergraduate grades and an aptitude
for law.

Job prospects as well as salaries are quite good for lawyers, so
if you have an interest in helping people through difficult times
in their lives, this may be the career for you.

Paralegals

If lawyers work late into the night, they are probably working
in tandem with paralegals. These people work under the direct
supervision of lawyers by investigating the facts, researching the
law, analyzing the information, and preparing reports for the
lawyer. Paralegals are there to assist the attorney during a trial
or in the preparation of legal documents. Just like lawyers, paralegals can also specialize in criminal, real estate, probate, corporate, tax, or international law.

You can become a paralegal by getting in-house training in
a law firm. This can happen through promotion from legal sec-
retary or from some other position that requires a college degree, such as research assistant. You can also get formal paralegal training in colleges, universities, law schools, and
community colleges. Usually you can complete the program in
two years, but programs and requirements will vary according
to your education and background.

You will take both general and specialized courses in real estate, probate, litigation, or criminal law. Computer courses are becoming necessary for all legal work now, too. Internships are also available through law firms, legal departments, and government agencies.

Although this occupation is only about 30 years old, it is growing steadily. Job prospects look good for the next several years, especially in private law firms. The average annual salary in 1991 was about $25,000, with the starting salary at about $21,000. Salaries will vary according to location and experience.

Support Staff

When the lawyers and paralegals are up all night working on a case, they will need support staff to process their work. Many large law firms have support staffs that work 24 hours a day, covering three shifts during that period. Clerical managers, word processors, and even print shop personnel may work around the clock with the attorneys.

Supervisors of the clerical staff make assignments, plan the work, and coordinate the work flow. They also act as liaison between their department and the lawyers and see to it that all equipment works.

Usually these supervisors train and evaluate the staff and make recommendations for promotions or demotions. They may also actively recruit new employees, test them, and interview them. They also schedule the staff, including vacations, sick and personal days, and assist in developing departmental policy and procedures.

Clerical supervisors have to keep personnel and other records, often are responsible for purchasing for the department, and have to keep up with the latest technology as it applies to the staff.

The supervisor, as well as the staff, may have a standard second or third shift or they may work a rotating shift. Those who work graveyard may do it because they prefer those hours. Others see it as a step toward the first shift, should an opening occur. Those who prefer it usually like the lack of rush-hour traffic and the ease of getting doctor and dentist appointments, just like other night owls.

Most supervisors come up through the ranks or from another department within the organization. You will have to demonstrate leadership, ability to work as a team member, be loyal to the organization, and have self-confidence. You should thoroughly understand the workings of your department and enjoy working with other people. You will also have to be able to motivate and encourage them.

One of the most essential support groups in a modern office is that of the computer or word processing operators. These skilled people are responsible for running the computer, printing the copy, loading the machine with disks and paper, and sometimes operating peripheral machines, such as modems and scanners. They generally have to keep records of work they have done and also of problems with the computers.

You can get computer training at four-year colleges, community colleges, or on the job. Sometimes manufacturers hold seminars, and if you have a military background, you may have learned the basics there. You might have to learn new procedures or software at each new job, depending on your experience. Since every office worker has to work with a computer at some time or other, you should start your training as early as possible. The ever-changing technology makes it important to maintain and expand your skills in order to take you into the future. Computers are here to stay, and they will become increasingly important in the age of cyberspace, Internet, infotainment, and e-mail. Your skills are important now, but they will be increasingly important on the information super highway.

Adult Education Teachers

Adult education teachers, who play an integral role in the education of a society, also work evenings and weekends. In some cases, they work in an office, plant, or factory during the day and then teach at night. They may not be out on the streets saving lives, but they perform a vital service in every community.

These teachers instruct in a wide variety of basic and technical skills, including reading, writing, math, electronics, foreign languages, dance, photography, computer science, and cooking. These and other courses prepare students for the General Educational Development Examination (GED), which is the high school equivalency test.

Many adult education teachers teach a trade or craft that they make their living from, such as hair dressing. Others are certified to teach a specialized course, such as Japanese. In some cases, a bachelor's degree will suffice for teaching adults; in others, a master's or doctorate is required. For some, a portfolio or samples of work will suffice. Certification is necessary in some states.

Adult education teachers have to keep up with the latest in educational methods and their own field by attending classes, seminars, conventions, and conferences.

Some of this education is necessary to supplement a student's high school education; in other cases, it is an introduction to a much needed job skill. In many cases, adult education teachers are involved in helping nonnative speakers learn the English language and American customs and culture.

For that reason, this country will continue to need adult education teachers in the near future. This is especially true for the basic GED and job enhancement skills courses and teaching English as a second language. You may advance to an administrative position or go into research, especially if you teach in a college or university.

To be a teacher, you will have to know your subject area thoroughly and be able to anticipate questions from your students. You must plan your lessons, leave time for grading papers, and know how to explain the subject so that everyone understands it.

You also need a passion for learning and an eagerness to pass on your knowledge to your students. In that way, you will also learn from them and begin to build a small community in the classroom with common goals and shared knowledge.

So, now that we have explored some possibilities for night owl careers, you need to take a good look at yourself, your capabilities, your aptitudes, your interests, your knowledge, and your experience to see where you might fit in best.

In most cases, you will have to be flexible, adaptable, reliable, and have a good sense of humor. For so many of these jobs, you will deal directly with a wide variety of people, so your customer service, public relations, and communications skills have to be highly developed.

For some night owl careers, you need to be sensitive to people's emotional and physical needs; for others, you will be responsible for their safety, comfort, and security. Still others will emphasize education and transmission of information. And luckily, some are there to entertain and amuse us.

For all, however, there will unfortunately be sleep deprivation, some eating irregularities, and a disrupted social life. But if you do what you love, these disadvantages won't matter. And besides, just remember—no rush hours!

For Further Information

American Association for Paralegal Education
P.O. Box 40244
Overland Park, KS 66204

American Association of Colleges of Pharmacy
1426 Prince St.
Alexandria, VA 22314

American Association of Hospital Pharmacists
4630 Montgomery Ave.
Bethesda, MD 20814

American Bakers Association
1111 14th St., NW
Suite 300
Washington, DC 20005

American Federation of Teachers
555 New Jersey Ave., NW
Washington, DC 20001

American Institute of Baking
1213 Bakers Way
Manhattan, KS 66502

Association of American Law Schools
1201 Connecticut Ave., NW
Suite 800
Washington, DC 20036

Direct Selling Association
1776 K St., NW
Suite 600
Washington, DC 20006

Graphic Arts Technical Foundation
4615 Forbes Ave.
Pittsburgh, PA 15213

Graphic Communications International Union
1900 L St., NW
Washington, DC 20036

Information Services
American Bar Association
750 North Lake Shore Dr.
Chicago, IL 60611

Institute for Certification of Computing Professionals
2200 East Devon Ave.
Suite 268
Des Plaines, IL 60018-4503

Law School Admissions Services
Box 2000
Newtown, PA 18940

National Association for Professional Saleswomen
1730 North Lynn St.
Suite 502
Arlington, VA 22209

National Association of Boards of Pharmacy
1300 Higgins Rd.
Suite 103
Park Ridge, IL 60068

National Association of Legal Assistants, Inc.
1601 Main St.
Suite 300
Tulsa, OK 74119

National Council for Accreditation of Teacher Education
2010 Massachusetts Ave., NW
Second Floor
Washington, DC 20036

National Education Association
1201 16th St. NW
Washington, DC 20036

National Federation of Paralegal Associations
Suite 201
104 Wilmot Rd.
Deerfield, IL 60015-5195

National Paralegal Association
P.O. Box 406
Solebury, PA 18963

National Retail Federation
100 West 31st St.
New York, NY 10001

Printing Industries of America
100 Daingerfield Rd.
Alexandria, VA 22314

Standing Committee on Legal Assistants
American Bar Association
750 North Lake Shore Dr.
Chicago, IL 60611

Acknowledgments and Additional Resources

Actors' Equity Association
165 West 46th St.
New York, NY 10036

Airline Pilots Association
1625 Massachusetts Ave., NW
Washington, DC 20036

Air Traffic Control Association, Inc.
James L. Crook
Vice President–Operations
2300 Clarendon Blvd.
Suite 711
Arlington, VA 22201

Air Transport Association of America
1709 New York Ave., NW
Washington, DC 20006

American Bus Association
1015 15th St., NW
Suite 250
Washington, DC 20005

The American Correctional Association
8025 Laurel Lakes Court
Laurel, MD 20707

American Dance Guild
33 West 21st St.
Third Floor
New York, NY 10010

American Federation of Musicians (Canada)
75 The Donway West
Suite 1010
Don Mills, Ontario
Canada M3C 2E9

American Federation of Musicians (U.S.)
1501 Broadway
Suite 600
Paramount Building
New York, NY 10036

American Guild of Musical Artists
1727 Broadway
New York, NY 10019-5284

American Hotel & Motel Association
1201 New York Ave., NW
Washington, DC 20005-3931

American Institute of Baking
Ronald Wirtz
Library Director
1213 Bakers Way
Manhattan KS 66502

The American Institute of Graphic Arts
1059 3rd Ave.
New York, NY 10021

American Jail Association
P.O. Box 2158
Hagerstown, MD 21742

American Newspaper Publishers Association Foundation
The Newspaper Center
Box 17407
Dulles International Airport
Washington, DC 20041

American Probation and Parole Association
P.O. Box 51017
Salt Lake City, UT 84152

American Public Transit Association
1201 New York Ave., NW
Suite 400
Washington, DC 20005

American Society of Magazine Editors
575 Lexington Ave.
New York, NY 10022

American Society of Magazine Photographers
419 Park Ave. South
New York, NY 10016

American Society of Newspaper Editors
Lee Stinnett
Executive Director
P.O. Box 4090
Reston, VA 22090-1700

American Symphony Orchestra League
Nena Manzo
Information Center Specialist
777 14th St., NW
Suite 500
Washington, DC 20005

American Trucking Associations
David. E. Garamella
Office of Public Affairs
2200 Mill Rd.
Alexandria, VA 22314-4677

Associated Actors and Artists of America
165 West 46th St.
New York, NY 10036

Associated Photographers International
5855 Green Valley Circle
Suite 109
Culver City, CA 90230

Association for Education in Journalism
and Mass Communications
University of South Carolina College of Journalism
1621 College St.
Columbia, SC 29208

Association of American Railroads
Office of Information and Public Affairs
50 F St., NW
Washington, DC 20001

Broadcast Education Association
National Association of Broadcasters
1771 N St., NW
Washington, DC 20036

Brotherhood of Locomotive Engineers
Stephen W. FitzGerald
Public Relations Director and Editor
Standard Building
Cleveland, OH 44113-1702

Communications Workers of America
1925 K St., NW
Washington, DC 20006

CONTAC, Inc.
P.O. Box 81826
Lincoln, NE 68501

Council on Hotel, Restaurant and Institutional Education
(CHRIE)
Deborah M. Romano
Coordinator, Information Services
Tara Hunter
Administrative Assistant
1200 17th St., NW
Washington, DC 20036-3097

The Dow Jones Newspaper Fund, Inc.
P.O. Box 300
Princeton, NJ 09543-0300

Eastman Kodak
Kodak Information Center
Department 841
343 State St.
Rochester, NY 14650

Federal Communications Commission
1919 M St., NW
Washington, DC 20554

Future Aviation Professionals of America
4959 Massachusetts Blvd.
Atlanta, GA 30337

Graphic Communications International Union
1900 L St., NW
Washington, DC 20036

Graphic Arts Technical Foundation
4615 Forbes Ave.
Pittsburgh, PA 15213

International Alliance of Theatrical Stage Employees and
Moving Picture Machine Operators of the United States and
Canada
1515 Broadway
Suite 601
New York, NY 10036

International Association of Fire Chiefs
1329 18th St., NW
Washington, DC 20036

International Association of Fire Fighters
1750 New York Ave., NW
Washington, DC 20006

International Union of Electronic, Electrical, Salaried,
Machine, and Furniture Workers
1126 16th St., NW
Washington, DC 20036

Music Educators National Conference
1902 Association Dr.
Reston, VA 22091

National Association of Broadcasters Employment Clearinghouse
1771 N St., NW
Washington, DC 20036

National Association of Schools of Dance
11250 Roger Bacon Dr.
Reston, VA 22090

National Association of Schools of Music
11250 Roger Bacon Dr.
Reston, VA 22091

National Association of Theatre Owners
4605 Lankershim Blvd.
Suite 340
North Hollywood, CA 91602-1891

National Cable Television Association
1724 Massachusetts Ave., NW
Washington, DC 20036

National Executive Housekeepers Association
1001 Eastwind Dr.
Suite 301
Westerville, OH 43081-3361

National Fire Protection Association
Batterymarch Park
Quincy, MA 02269

National Highway Traffic Safety Administration
U.S. Department of Transportation
NTS-22
400 7th St., SW
Washington, DC 20590

National Newspaper Association
1627 K St., NW
Suite 400
Washington, IL 20006

National Railroad Passenger Corp.
60 Massachusetts Ave., NE
Washington, DC 20002

National Restaurant Association
Susan Pratt
Librarian
Technical Services
1200 Seventh St., NW
Washington, DC 20036-3097

National Retail Foundation
100 West 31st St.
New York, NY 10001

Newspaper Careers Project
The Newspaper Center
11600 Sunrise Valley Dr.
Reston, VA 22091

The Newspaper Guild
David J. Eisen
Director
Research & Information
8611 Second Ave.
Silver Spring, MD 20910

Printing Industries of America
Terry L. Harris
Association Relations Manager
100 Daingerfield Rd.
Alexandria, VA 22314

Professional Photographers of America, Inc.
1090 Executive Way
Des Plaines, IL 60018

Radio-Television News Directors Association
1717 K St., NW
Suite 615
Washington, DC 20006

Santa Fe Pacific Corporation
Public Relations
224 South Michigan Ave.
Chicago, IL, 60604-2401

Society of Broadcast Engineers
7002 Graham Rd.
Suite 216
Indianapolis, IN 46220

The Society of Illustrators
128 East 63rd St.
New York, NY 10021

The Society of Publication Designers
60 East 42nd St.
Suite 1416
New York, NY 10165

U.S. Department of Transportation
Alfredia G. Brooks
Personnel Staffing Specialist
Federal Aviation Administration
800 Independence Ave., SW
Washington, DC 20591

United States Telephone Association
900 19th St., NW
Suite 800
Washington, DC 20006

Richard Valdez, Graphic Artist
Technical Consultant

VGM CAREER BOOKS

CAREER DIRECTORIES
Careers Encyclopedia
Dictionary of Occupational
  Titles
Occupational Outlook
  Handbook

CAREERS FOR
Animal Lovers
Bookworms
Computer Buffs
Crafty People
Culture Lovers
Environmental Types
Film Buffs
Foreign Language
  Aficionados
Good Samaritans
Gourmets
History Buffs
Kids at Heart
Nature Lovers
Night Owls
Number Crunchers
Shutterbugs
Sports Nuts
Travel Buffs

CAREERS IN
Accounting; Advertising;
Business; Child Care;
Communications;
Computers; Education;
Engineering; Finance;
Government; Health Care;
High Tech; Journalism; Law;
Marketing; Medicine;
Science; Social &
Rehabilitation Services

CAREER PLANNING
Admissions Guide to
  Selective Business Schools
Beginning Entrepreneur
Career Planning &
  Development for College
  Students & Recent
  Graduates
Career Change

Careers Checklists
Cover Letters They Don't
  Forget
Executive Job Search
  Strategies
Guide to Basic Cover Letter
  Writing
Guide to Basic Resume
  Writing
Joyce Lain Kennedy's Career
  book
Out of Uniform
Slam Dunk Resumes
Successful Interviewing for
  College Seniors

CAREER PORTRAITS
Animals
Music
Sports
Teaching

GREAT JOBS FOR
English Majors
Foreign Language Majors
History Majors
Psychology Majors

HOW TO
Approach an Advertising
  Agency and Walk Away
  with the Job You Want
Bounce Back Quickly After
  Losing Your Job
Change Your Career
Choose the Right Career
Find Your New Career Upon
  Retirement
Get & Keep Your First Job
Get Hired Today
Get into the Right Law
  School
Have a Winning Job Interview
Hit the Ground Running in
  Your New Job
Improve Your Study Skills
Jump Start a Stalled Career
Land a Better Job

Launch Your Career in TV
  News
Make the Right Career Moves
Market Your College Degree
Move from College into a
  Secure Job
Negotiate the Raise You
  Deserve
Prepare a *Curriculum Vitae*
Prepare for College
Run Your Own Home
  Business
Succeed in College
Succeed in High School
Write a Winning Resume
Write Successful Cover
  Letters
Write Term Papers & Reports
Write Your College
  Application Essay

OPPORTUNITIES IN
This extensive series provides
detailed information on
nearly 150 individual career
fields.

RESUMES FOR
Advertising Careers
Banking and Financial
  Careers
Business Management
  Careers
College Students &
  Recent Graduates
Communications Careers
Education Careers
Engineering Careers
Environmental Careers
Health and Medical Careers
High School Graduates
High Tech Careers
Midcareer Job Changes
Sales and Marketing Careers
Scientific and Technical
  Careers
Social Service Careers
The First-Time Job Hunter

VGM Career Horizons
a division of *NTC Publishing Group*
4255 West Touhy Avenue
Lincolnwood, Illinois 60646-1975

Date Due

Nov 3			

BRODART, INC.   Cat. No. 23 233   Printed in U.S.A.